100+ Fun Ideas for

Teaching Boys in Primary School

Visual, Kinaesthetic and Competitive Activities to Help Boys Achieve their Potential

Mark McEvilly

Brilliant
PUBLICATIONS

We hope you and your pupils enjoy using the ideas in this book. Listed below are a few of our other books which might be of interest to you. Information on these and all our other books can be found on our website: www.brilliantpublications.co.uk.

100+ Fun Ideas for Practising MFL in the Primary Classroom
More Fun Ideas for Advancing MFL in the Primary Classroom
Creative Homework Tasks, 7–9 Year Olds
Creative Homework Tasks, 9–11 Year Olds
Team-building Activities for Key Stage 1
Team-building Activities for Key Stage 2
Thinking Strategies for the Successful Classroom, 5–7 Year Olds
Thinking Strategies for the Successful Classroom, 7–9 Year Olds
Thinking Strategies for the Successful Classroom, 9–11 Year Olds

Published by Brilliant Publications
Unit 10
Sparrow Hall Farm
Edlesborough
Dunstable
Bedfordshire
LU6 2ES, UK

www.brilliantpublications.co.uk

The name Brilliant Publications and the logo are registered trademarks.

Written by Mark McEvilly
Illustrated by Frank Endersby
Cover illustration by Catherine Ward

© Text Mark McEvilly 2011
© Design Brilliant Publications 2011
Printed ISBN 978-1-905780-83-9
ebook ISBN 978-0-85747-138-3
First printed and published in the UK in 2011

Contents

Introduction   10

No.	Activity	V	A	K	T	C	H	Page no.
Visual teaching ideas *General*								
1	Visual word games	▪				▪		19
2	Pictorial activities	▪						21
3	Presenting facts	▪	▪		▪			22
4	Advertising	▪					▪	22
5	Structure grids	▪						23
6	Classification keys	▪		▪				23
7	Quick quiz	▪				▪		24
8	Freeze frame	▪						24
9	Kim's game	▪				▪		24
10	Encyclopedic entry	▪						25
11	Topic book	▪			▪		▪	25
Literacy								
12	Visual literacy skills	▪				▪		26
13	Create a dictionary	▪					▪	27
14	Word banks	▪						28
15	Book review	▪						28
16	Character grids	▪	▪					29
17	Character work	▪			▪			30
18	Inspiring creative writing	▪	▪					31
19	Information book sections	▪			▪		▪	33
20	Reports and reviews	▪	▪		▪	▪		34
21	Newspaper headline: sort and match	▪				▪		35
22	Newspaper/web news comparison	▪					▪	35
23	Comparative news	▪	▪		▪		▪	36
24	Film education	▪		▪				36

Key: V = Visual; A = Auditory; K = Kinaesthetic; T = Team; C = Competitive; H = Higher order learning activity

No.	Activity	V	A	K	T	C	H	Page no.
25	Media and plays	■	■				■	37
26	Ticket design	■						37
27	Posters	■					■	38
28	Picture that!	■			■			39
29	Show me							40
30	Role-playing		■					40
31	Giving instructions	■		■	■			41
32	Digital storyboard	■					■	42
33	Hyperlink PowerPoint	■					■	42
34	Different perspectives	■					■	43
Numeracy								
35	Play your cards right	■	■		■			44
36	Co-ordinates symmetrical mask	■		■				44
37	Digital root patterns	■					■	45
38	Times tables graphs	■						46
39	Roman times tables	■						46
40	Ancient Egyptian multiplication	■					■	47
Science								
41	Line graph narrative	■					■	48
42	Recount	■	■					48
History								
43	History pictorial activities	■					■	49
44	Historical maps	■					■	50
45	House comparison							51
46	Rich/poor comparison chart							51
47	TV news			■	■			52
48	When they were young							52
49	Personal and class timelines	■					■	53
50	Historical timetable	■					■	53
51	Alphabets	■	■			■		54
52	Scribe a letter	■					■	54

Key: V = Visual; A = Auditory; K = Kinaesthetic; T = Team; C = Competitive; H = Higher order learning activity

No.	Activity	V	A	K	T	C	H	Page no.
Geography								
53	Local or world/national picture maps	■						55
54	Virtual maps	■		■			■	56
55	Sports map	■						57
56	Task map	■						57
57	Choropleth map	■					■	58
58	Identifying key features	■						59
59	Photo record	■						60
60	Holiday destinations	■						60
61	Estate agent	■					■	61
62	Cloud survey	■						61
63	Micro water cycle	■		■				62
64	Global food	■		■				62
MFL								
65	Symbol and word match cards	■			■			63
66	Body and clothes beetle drive	■	■	■				64
RE								
67	Prayer	■						65
PSHE								
68	Action	■		■	■			66
69	Role models	■		■				67
70	Positive words	■	■				■	68
71	Personal timetable	■						68
72	Visual healthy menu	■						69
73	Lifestyle map	■					■	69
Kinaesthetic teaching ideas *General*								
74	Mime			■	■			70
75	Instructions			■			■	71
76	Thought lines			■				71
77	Name game	■		■		■		72

Key: V = Visual; A = Auditory; K = Kinaesthetic; T = Team; C = Competitive; H = Higher order learning activity

No.	Activity	V	A	K	T	C	H	Page no.
78	Secret whiteboards	■		■		■		72
79	Getting out of the classroom			■				73
80	3-D Carroll diagrams	■					■	74
81	Sorting ideas	■				■		75
82	Sequencing	■		■	■			76
83	Washing line	■		■	■			76

Literacy

No.	Activity	V	A	K	T	C	H	Page no.
84	Fun spelling			■				77
85	Tactile words	■		■				78
86	Adjective word bank			■			■	78
87	Role-play		■	■			■	79
88	Student sculpture			■				79
89	Mr Men™ books						■	80
90	Book swap circle	■			■			80
91	Product review	■		■				81
92	Model making	■		■			■	82
93	Investigating characters			■	■			83
94	Lost	■	■	■	■		■	84

Numeracy

No.	Activity	V	A	K	T	C	H	Page no.
95	Shape maths	■		■	■		■	85
96	Team angles			■	■			86
97	Shape creation			■				86
98	Kinaesthetic patterns	■		■				87
99	Times table stand up factors			■		■	■	88
100	Magic chairs	■		■	■			88
101	Fractions	■		■				89
102	Step estimation			■				90
103	Team clocks			■	■		■	90
104	Axis co-ordinates Twister®			■		■	■	91

Science

No.	Activity	V	A	K	T	C	H	Page no.
105	Transparent, translucent and opaque				■			92
106	Life-sized paper skeleton			■				93

Key: V = Visual; A = Auditory; K = Kinaesthetic; T = Team; C = Competitive; H = Higher order learning activity

No.	Activity	V	A	K	T	C	H	Page no.
107	Earth, Moon and Sun			■	■			94
108	Exploring nature			■				95
109	Junior field studies			■				97
History								
110	Kinaesthetic history ideas	■		■			■	98
111	What really happened?		■	■	■		■	99
Geography								
112	Inflatable globes			■				100
113	Geography Twister®			■				101
114	Compass bearings			■				101
115	International sign posts	■		■				102
MFL								
116	Kinaesthetic MFL ideas	■	■	■				102
117	MFL Twister®	■	■	■		■		103
RE								
118	Physical prayer			■			■	103
PE								
119	Instant PE lesson			■			■	104
120	PE science			■				105
PSHE								
121	Friendly words	■		■				105
Competitive teaching ideas *General*								
122	Team raps and poems		■			■		106
123	Topic singing		■		■	■		106
124	Mistakes		■			■		107
125	Word and time boundary	■				■		107
126	Speaking challenges		■			■		108
127	Hot seat mind map		■			■		109
128	Listening, writing and speaking games	■	■			■		110
129	Name hat		■		■	■		111
Literacy								
130	Word pairs		■			■		112

Key: V = Visual; A = Auditory; K = Kinaesthetic; T = Team; C = Competitive; H = Higher order learning activity

No.	Activity	V	A	K	T	C	H	Page no.
131	Book team	✓				✓		113
132	Land's End to John O'Groats reading race	✓				✓		114
133	Races	✓				✓		116
134	Secret definition		✓			✓	✓	116
135	Envoy				✓	✓		117

Numeracy

No.	Activity	V	A	K	T	C	H	Page no.
136	Football pitch multiplication	✓				✓		118
137	Physical pairs			✓				119
138	Number line: connect 3	✓						119

MFL

No.	Activity	V	A	K	T	C	H	Page no.
139	MFL ideas	✓	✓			✓		120
140	MFL noughts and crosses	✓				✓		121
141	Numbers, colours, shapes and letters	✓	✓	✓				121
142	Colour 'fruit'	✓	✓			✓	✓	122
143	MFL faces	✓	✓			✓		122
144	Last man standing		✓			✓		123

Geography

No.	Activity	V	A	K	T	C	H	Page no.
145	Map symbol snap	✓				✓		124
146	Treasure hunt			✓				124

PE

No.	Activity	V	A	K	T	C	H	Page no.
147	Magic stick		✓	✓	✓			125
148	Roll out			✓	✓			126

PSHE

No.	Activity	V	A	K	T	C	H	Page no.
149	Head down, thumbs up		✓	✓		✓		127

Higher order thinking skills

General

No.	Activity	V	A	K	T	C	H	Page no.
150	Setting goals and providing feedback		✓				✓	128
151	Speaking games		✓		✓		✓	129
152	Group discussion		✓		✓		✓	130
153	Questions		✓		✓	✓	✓	131
154	Board game			✓				131

Key: V = Visual; A = Auditory; K = Kinaesthetic; T = Team; C = Competitive; H = Higher order learning activity

No.	Activity	V	A	K	T	C	H	Page no.
Literacy								
155	Storytelling and debating		■		■	■	■	132
156	Soundtrack		■				■	133
157	Gathering information				■		■	133
158	Fact, opinion or belief?	■					■	134
159	Ask the author		■				■	134
160	Text discussion		■				■	135
161	Personal responses		■				■	136
162	Wrong reading	■	■				■	136
163	Prediction		■		■		■	137
164	Alternative scene		■	■		■	■	137
165	Alternative versions		■	■				138
166	Get to know your character	■	■	■			■	139
167	Creative writing starting points	■	■	■	■		■	141
Numeracy								
168	Market research	■	■	■	■		■	143
Geography								
169	Local improvements	■					■	144
170	Urban v rural	■					■	144
171	PE map	■		■			■	145
172	Playground map	■	■	■			■	146
History								
173	What happens next?		■		■		■	147
174	Rules		■				■	147
175	Past lives		■				■	148
176	Topical music		■				■	148
RE								
177	Our prayer		■		■		■	149
PSHE								
178	Goal setting	■					■	149

Key: V = Visual; A = Auditory; K = Kinaesthetic; T = Team; C = Competitive; H = Higher order learning activity

Subject index   150

Introducton

The male mind

We don't teach generic children. Each is a unique individual. In fact, according to neuroscientists there may not even be a human brain at all. Instead we may have to rediscover that we teach two different brains: male and female, both made from markedly different DNA leading to numerous variations in chemistry and wiring of the 'wet-wear' circuitry. Neurobiologists have now tracked over 100 differences between female and male brains (Gurian, 2009).

This highly complex organ exclusively contains 6,000 of our 30,000 genes that are utilized nowhere else in the human body. Magnetic resonance imaging is used to monitor and explore the brain as it functions, allowing us to increasingly view the operating of the mind. Brain imaging techniques, for instance, can scan the brain showing how different parts of the organ light up local neurons. These can record how brains function during different activities or even when focused upon different thoughts. Imaging a familiar face or a familiar place activates different parts of the same brain. Similar technology, such as TMS (trans-cranial-magnetic-stimulation) and fMRI (functional Magnetic Resonance Imaging), can be used to measure and compare brain activity and structure during various mental states.

Other recent discoveries have unlocked the biological evidence between the rates and sequence with which brain development occurs in both boys and girls. 'In 2007, the world's largest study of brain development in children published their most comprehensive study to date, demonstrating that there is no overlap in the trajectories of brain development in girls and boys' (NASSPE: 2010).

Brain structure differences

We don't underestimate the differences between adult men and women. We accommodate and appreciate those differences seeing them as part of the uniqueness and qualities of the individual. During the 1970s, however, Western educationalists became increasingly influenced by two notions. The first was a legitimate desire to eradicate barriers holding girls back from pursuing future careers in traditionally masculine fields. The second, that most gender differences were in fact environmental constructs by society (historically used to oppress women) and could therefore be discarded. It was believed that nurture and not nature was the predominate cause of gender variation. The brain itself was presumed to be the same for both sexes. This is now known to be wrong.

The variation in genetic blueprints for both sets of human brains, are enormous with considerable anatomical differences.

Male brain	Female brain
Larger parietal cortex (processes signals from sensory organs and spatial perception)	Larger frontal lobe (decision making and problem solving)
Larger amygdala (controls emotions, social and sexual behaviour)	Larger limbic cortex (regulates emotion)
More testosterone (secreted by the brain)	Larger hippocampus (short term memory)
	Larger corpus callosum (connecting the left and right hemispheres of the brain)
	More serotonin (a neurotransmitter that inhibits aggression)
Enriched connections within right hemisphere of brain	Enriched connections between right and left hemispheres

Adapted (Hoag: New Scientist, 19 July 2008)

Simply put, the left hemisphere controls thinking and the right hemisphere controls spatial–physical relationships. In experiments when males and females have been asked to recall emotional images, males utilized the right side of the amygdala (part of the brain) and the females the left. Both groups also remembered different elements of the image. Females focused upon the details and males upon the overview of the situation.

Rubin Gur at the University of Pennsylvania uses brain scan equipment to record areas of activity within the brain whilst it completes certain tasks. He then records the intensity with which the brain is utilizing different parts of its structure. During spatial activities the males utilized the right hemisphere to a far greater degree than the females. This is why males often do better at spatial activities from Lego to architecture. By comparison, female brains having greater left/right hemisphere linkage are able to draw more upon both sides of the brain at once which is required for tasks such as reading and identifying emotion. Male brains are known to activate to complete a task and then switch down into 'stand-by', whilst females brains remain 'always on' (Gurian 1996).

Hearing

Teachers are often frustrated when pupils, especially boys, don't listen. A reason that boys may not hear is not due to lax discipline but biology. Males have better hearing generally in one ear than the other. It could be worth discovering which ear is dominant and seating pupils accordingly. Boys are less able than girls to pick out background noises and also less able to detect differences in voice inference or other emotional data.

Boys brains are less adept at processing auditory data than girls. Displaying visual instructions, references etc, could be a more effective way to gain their attention. Utilizing artefacts, games or body movement when possible helps to establish mental connections with the task at hand (Frean 2008).

Sight

In a similar way to one ear being dominant, boys often see more effectively with their left eye since this leads directly to the right hemisphere of the brain, a male's strongest side. Boys are often geared toward skills associated with hunting and tracking. This historical orientation still leads to males engaging in spatial activity that is highly physical and visual. One of the reasons for the popularity of computer games with males of all ages is the opportunity to explore a virtual environment and utilize actual eye–hand physical skills. This visual-spatial co-ordination can also explain why males may be more

Teaching Boys in Primary School

successful in abstract spatial constructs, such as those found within mathematics.

Hormones and physiologies

Testosterone is the dominant male hormone that is responsible for higher levels of aggression and competitiveness. As boys get older, sexual drive and increased muscle mass may also become apparent. Michael Gurian identifies three behaviour patterns in boys fuelled by testosterone and guided by male brain wiring:

✦ The search for instant or quick gratification, whether in eating quickly, or jumping from activity to activity
✦ The tendency to move quickly to problem solving, even in emotionally complex experiences
✦ The tendency to find activities through which his body will build physical tension – like sports or other concentrated, single task experiences (Gurian 1996).

With too much to do in the classroom already how can we ensure that the current weaker of these two groups is not let down any further whilst not demanding the impossible of teaching staff? This book, I hope, can make a contribution to closing the gender gap.

Big ideas for working with boys

Competition

Why are boys often competitive? Testosterone, which is between 10 to 20 times higher in adolescent males than females, accounts for the difference. For boys, competition is also a part of nurturing, encouraging each other to achieve their full potential rather than ignoble ease, something that too many males fall easily into. Males can bolster their self-image through healthy balanced competition which reveals their strengths (Gurian 1996: 33).

In their adult lives for which nature is preparing them, they will face competition for the right mate, career and other hierarchical systems in society. Attempting to ignore or dissuade this reality is foolish and glosses over the reality of life which boys and their peers are already aware of.

Sports and games of many kinds whether physical or strategic (Warhammer table-top or computer games etc) bring boys together to grow and nurture through competition.

Within this book are a number of ideas for including an element of competition within the lesson. This can take a number of forms that could be utilized across the school day and implemented as an ongoing strategy to engage male learners.

Spatial and physical

In traditional societies, whether hunter/gatherer or agrarian/industrial, males have developed roles that honour their natural brain and muscular wiring towards physical tasks. We cannot simply activate an off switch during the school day that denies the reality of their biology and brain chemistry. Whilst as educators we have every right to expect and enforce positive learning attitudes and behaviours we may gain the best results through working with, rather than against physical movement (McClure 2008: 71).

Building in a degree of physical movement, where practical, honours this need and may well provide what Gurian refers to as a 'brain break', giving the boy's brain an opportunity to focus, process and re-energize. For pupils who are particularly kinaesthetic, during times where they are required to sit at their desks and watch, write or listen, provide them with a squeeze ball. For such learners, allowing their brain to utilize its highly physical focus may help them to concentrate on the task at hand.

Team work

In traditional cultures males were often required to work as part of teams in pursuit of shared goals, whether food, security or exploring new ground. Group work can be effective in harnessing male energy to engage boys in learning if planned well. For these learning groups or teams to be effective there needs to be:

- ✦ Planned complimentary roles within the group
- ✦ A clearly defined task or goal for the team to achieve together
- ✦ Time for collectively reflecting and listening to each other to create an agreed group result.

Ensure that the above are securely put in place to prevent purposeless groups turning into competitive forums where members compete against each other rather than collaborate together.

Less writing: more visual and kinaesthetic work

As Wilson (2007) so clearly comments, many hindrances to boys' educational progress are connected to writing. Many intelligent, energized, curious and enthusiastic learners are discouraged or even switched off by excessive writing that is sometimes expected by educationalists, seemingly, to the boy's eyes, without purpose.

Knowing that a high degree of aural and written fluency is a life skill, as well as an examination requirement, how do we harness the many high energy positives into practical educational progress?

Practical implementation

The following seven pointers help me when planning, or even if I have to adapt a lesson in full flow, depending upon both boys' and girls' learning needs.

- ✦ **VAK (visual, auditory, kinaesthetic) planning**
  When reading through existing planning, jot down or annotate on the planning pages whether the activities are VAK. With this easy-to-scan overview, you can see if you will be providing a varied, balanced learning diet to keep the class healthy and engaged. Ideally, try to include an element of all three styles in every lesson if possible. To help in planning, the Contents list indicates the various learning styles each idea encourages.

✦ Balance

Not every lesson needs to be 'all singing, all dancing'. Boys, like girls, need to accept that there will be times when we all have to settle to a task, regardless of personal preferences. No doubt it is also character developing for children to realize this, since it will certainly be true in the world of work. As a teacher you also work long and often stressful hours. Give yourself a break. If an occasional lesson is simple or traditional, it won't jeopardize your boys' future.

✦ Girls

Girls also benefit from variety in learning and teaching styles. Some individual girls may directly benefit from new stimuli that may suit them better as individuals. They may develop better communication skills from team or competitive tasks. Extending exposure to visual, technological and kinaesthetic skills could also encourage and unleash large volumes of untapped female potential in the classroom, that more staid teaching has yet to unlock.

✦ Behaviour

Think about the proportion of your time that is spent resolving disruption, whether low level or more aggressive. In most classrooms significantly more time is spent resolving behaviour with boys than any similar issues with girls. If the boys in your classroom are engaged, leading to less disruption within the classroom, then it may contribute to girls learning by default. Less time spent getting boys on task equals more time spent teaching children of both sexes.

✦ Life-long learners

All of our children will have to adapt to technology and work roles that have yet to be created. Making independent choices using a broad variety of tools applies to all 21st century children and future adults. Why not allow them to operate, when appropriate, in a more 'real life' environment using real work tools and skills. Allow them to choose how to respond, eg PowerPoint, 3-D labelled model, role-play, pod cast, video newscast etc. Surely this is more appropriate to real working skills, than yet another essay/written question type response?

✦ **Integrating ideas into lessons**
The ideas in this book are often only a single idea for part of a lesson. They may help provide an attention grabbing introduction or be part of a broader task. They need not dominate the entire lesson. Use the ideas to create a balanced diet of learning within your planning. Use them for short-term assessment or feedback partway through a lesson to see how pupils are progressing.

✦ **Quick fixes**
We all experience a lesson that may not achieve all that was planned. A class may need calming or livening up. Many of the more generic ideas can often be applied rapidly with no preparation other than some fresh thinking. A simple lively task to change direction or a strong plenary can rescue the situation. Dip into the general ideas at the start of each chapter to have two or three cards up your sleeve.

How to use this book

Contents
The Contents lists ideas in the order they appear in the book. They are grouped under learning styles first: visual, kinaesthetic, competitive and higher order. Each learning style is then subdivided into the most relevant subject area: general, literacy, numeracy, science, history, geography, MFL, RE, PE and PSHE. (This is not exhaustive and you may find it helpful to dip into the index at the back to view additional uses for the ideas.)

Index
Within the Index, ideas are grouped alphabetically under subject headings. Many ideas have multiple applications and appear more than once, and not just under one subject.

Ideas

If you wish to share any ideas for possible inclusion within future editions of this book, feel free to send them to: ideas4teachingboys@gmail.com.

Best wishes and enjoy teaching.

Mark McEvilly

References

Frean, Alexandra (2008) Boys, brains and toxic lessons, [Online]. Available: http://www.timesonline.co.uk/tol/news/uk/education/article3234354.ece [7 July 2010]

Gurian, Michael (2009) The Purpose of Boys: Helping our sons find meaning, significance, and direction in their lives, San Francisco: Jossey-Bass

Gurian, Michael (1996) The Wonder of Boys, New York: Tarcher/Putnam

Hoag, Hannah (2008) Sex on the brain, New Scientist: 19 July 2008, 28-31

McClure, Ali (2008) Making it Better for Boys, in Schools, Families and Communities London: Continuum

Newland, Martin (2008) 'The Betrayal of Boys', Daily Mail, 24 July p.56-57

Useful articles

Some useful on-line articles are available in plain English that can provide more information than is available in this introduction:
www.scientificamerican.com/article.cfm?id=girl-brain-boy-brain
www.sciencedaily.com/releases/2008/03/080303120346.htm
www.singlesexschools.org/research-brain.htm
www.boysadrift.com/2007Giedd.pdf
www.timesonline.co.uk/tol/news/uk/education/article3234354.ece

Teaching Boys in Primary School

General

1. Visual word games

What you need: pens, paper, whiteboard, dictionaries
Subject links: any

✦ ACROSTIC POEMS
  Write about any topic in the form of an acrostic to help
  reinforce subject vocabulary, rules, facts etc. If individual
  words are not easily applicable, short lines of verse referring
  to relevant facts and containing the relevant letter can be
  utilized instead.

✦ ANAGRAMS
  Based upon a shared topic, pupils should make up their
  own anagrams. Write them on the class whiteboard. The
  competition is to decode them all in the fastest time.
  Winners are those with the most challenging and fastest
  decoding. Declare any records for each word and overall
  winners.

✦ CROSSWORDS AND CROSSNUMBERS
  Pupils create their own crosswords with questions devised
  from a topic. Emphasize the need for accuracy and
  challenge. Blank grids of squared paper provide the most
  flexibility. After pupils have written their initial answers in
  approximately one third of the squares, they should shade in
  the remaining squares.

✦ MISSING WORDS
  Similar to a cloze exercise, this can be completed either
  without the missing words provided at all (pupils should use
  a dictionary, thesaurus or glossary), or as a differentiated
  cloze exercise.

✦   WORD SEARCH
A useful calming activity. Utilizing relevant topic
terminology, the class create word searches on grids of
square paper. Pupils may either be supported using a word
bank or encouraged to investigate and check spellings
for more challenging words linked to the topic. Hold
a competition to create the most challenging, fiendish
word search. Enforce a time limit to complete production,
followed by a timed contest once word searches have been
exchanged. The teacher should referee while searches are
created if pupils are unsure if a word is directly relevant or
not.

✦   Traditionally, a complete list of the hidden words is recorded
beside the grid itself. For a greater challenge some word
searches could be made harder by NOT including the list,
although restricting the hidden words to a specific subtopic.

2. **Pictorial activities**

What you need: whiteboard, pens, pencils, paper. For Captions, assorted relevent images

Subject links: any

✦ CAPTIONS
Show pupils an image. Pupils then write an appropriate caption for this image. This may be best prepared on a worksheet or may be written on personal whiteboards in pairs or larger groups in a competitive format for class display. Pupils' art work can be used for the images. The captions may also be developed further into opening sentences and paragraphs for each image, or used as prompts for oral recount.

✦ PICTIONARY
Pupils should be divided into teams of mixed predominant learning styles for this visual exercise. The teacher or pupil(s) should draw an object or artefact from a topic studied. The rest of the class or team(s) then have to guess what it is. Prepare a list of appropriate topic related subjects that are to be drawn. Points are awarded for guessing the correct answer in the shortest possible time.

✦ STORY MAP
Pupils draw a map of a story or event. This engages all their recollection and communication skills through visual means. This is NOT an art picture. Instead, draw using stick people, sketches and symbols, all appropriate for retelling and recalling the story.

3. **Presenting facts**

What you need: topic books and/or Internet access. For Factual Video, any relevent television or Internet video
Subject links: any

✦ FACTUAL VIDEO
Watch a TV or Internet video. Children should make notes with the aim of reporting back to others in the class. You could divide the class into teams with different teams watching different media if possible.

✦ PRESENTATION
Using books, the Internet or artefacts, pupils should explore a subtopic of their own choice for 10–20 minutes. Do not encourage writing unless they wish to take notes. They then feedback to the rest of the class within a time limit what they have found out. They could show and tell about artefacts, use the interactive white board, or sketch/mime or model to communicate their discoveries.

4. **Advertising**

What you need: pens, paper
Subject links: any

✦ Create an advertisement to appear in a magazine promoting a useful product, skill or topic, eg a Roman road building company, promoting the use of division in everyday life, location studied in history/geography for holidays, etc.

✦ ICT could be used in PowerPoint presentations.

5. Structure grids

What you need: pre-drawn grids, on both whiteboard and worksheets
Subject links: literacy, science, RE, PSHE, history, geography

✦ Ideal for factual texts, although the grids may also be used for character or plot analysis. Map content onto double column grid structures, eg evidence grids contrasting points for and against an argument, cause and effect grids, argument and counter argument grids.

Reasons FOR invading Britain	Reasons AGAINST invading Britain

6. Classification keys

What you need: optional card, string, pens
Subject links: any

✦ Create classification keys not only for ideas in science but also to identify characters from a text, countries and locations, types of sport, members of the class, healthy foods, etc. To keep the key simple, have only two options to each question within the key.

✦ To make this exercise more kinaesthetic, and to enable corrections to be made more easily, write down all the questions on cards and link the answers together with string. This would encourage some learners to physically trace their responses. If practical, glue an actual sample of the classified object at the end of each chain, eg types of leaf.

7. Quick quiz

What you need: pupils' own whiteboards and pens
Subject links: any

✦ Create 10 fast questions as an introduction or plenary. Link them to previous learning. For visual responses use pupils' own whiteboards to ensure that all participate.

✦ Accept written, drawn or dramatized responses, allowing pupils to decide with which learning style they respond. Sketches could include maps, diagrams, charts, emblems, etc.

8. Freeze frame

What you need: existing text or video footage
Subject links: RE, literacy, geography, history, PSHE

✦ Either read a dramatic extract building up to an event or show a 30 second video clip. Pupils then use existing knowledge, evidence or imagination to describe what happens next, eg the start of a volcanic eruption. Pupils could use writing frames or labelled illustrations to support their ideas.

9. Kim's game

What you need: artefacts, tray, cloth, paper, pens
Subject links: history, RE, geography, speaking and listening

✦ This activity is named after Rudyard Kipling's Kim. Fill a tray with artefacts or objects belonging to a topic. Give the class a certain amount of time to see and to remember the objects. Cover the tray over with a cloth. Pupils must then write down what objects they saw, as well as how or what they were used for etc. Focus upon achieving the correct spellings as well.

10. Encyclopedic entry

What you need: prior pupil subject knowledge, reference sources
Subject links: history, geography, RE, science, literacy

✦ Write an entry for an encyclopedia based upon any aspect, object or character from the topic. Wikipedia is a useful model as there is a simple English version. (This is found on left-hand tool bar near the entry field.) Display the online encyclopedia on the whiteboard and encourage pupils to suggest entries that can then be explored.

11. Topic book

What you need: information texts or websites
Subject links: any

✦ The specific outcome of this activity is a topic book of work written in different genres. Pupils can then celebrate a completed, large-scale project and see how their writing is contributing to a broad-ranging, high-quality learning resource.

✦ For example, using any geographical, religious or historical resource, produce a book with a travelogue feature describing a location, instructions for a task, a first-person diary account, a third-person newspaper article, a simple role-play of an event, relevant poem, menu, letter to or from one of the characters, etc.

Literacy

12.   Visual literacy skills

What you need: For Highlight and Summarize, selected text and highlighters. For Scanning, copies of suitable pages from newspaper (1 page from TV/radio and one news page). For Venn Diagram Word Sort, word cards (or sticky notes), circles (on whiteboards, formed by string, hula hoops, etc).

Subject links: literacy

✦   HIGHLIGHT AND SUMMARIZE
Highlight either key words or sentences in each paragraph. Summarize each paragraph using one or two key words. Create overviews of text by displaying in another prose format, such as a labelled picture or diagram, word web, comparison chart, story map, etc.

✦   SCANNING
This exercise will help to improve speed and the ability to scan text. Give a copy of the pages to each pupil. (I keep suitable pages for future use.) Ask a set of prepared questions to discover facts from the text, using a stopwatch to time pupils. Possible questions could include: 'In which city will it be 20 degrees today?'; 'What is the name of the person involved in X?'; 'Which radio station will be DJed by X?' Record the fastest names and times on the board in a league table.

✦   VENN DIAGRAM WORD SORT
Sort words into the correct categories (adjectives, adverbs, past, future tenses, etc). This could be timed as a race and differentiated by the complexity of the words used. Using words from a topic could emphasize the practical relevance and application of the topic knowledge.

13. Create a dictionary

What you need: awareness of the language used in topic studied, reference books
Subject links: science, RE, history, geography, PSHE, MFL

✦ For any topic involving a number of terms unfamiliar to the class, help them to expand their accurate use of the new vocabulary by creating their own picture dictionary. For clarity, write the original word in a different colour. Define the word type (noun, adjective etc) and write a brief concise definition.

✦ Ensure space is left for appropriate illustrations to be added after written entries are completed. A visual image will help reinforce the meaning and use of the topic vocabulary.

Castle (noun)

Moat (noun)

Defend (verb)

Rampart (noun)

14. **Word banks**

What you need: sticky notes, pens, pencils, paper
Subject links: literacy

✦ GLOSSARIES
Expand pupils' word power by gathering lists of words of whose meanings they are unsure. Pupils can then create their own glossaries to explain the key vocabulary of a topic.

✦ STICKY NOTES
Give pupils a set of words studied in a topic. Pupils write clearly any words that they are uncertain of onto sticky notes. Groups or the class can then discuss strategies for decoding the meaning of the word, eg root, prefix, etc. The meaning and any visual aids could be recorded on the sticky notes to create a short-term word bank useful for that topic or group of lessons.

✦ TEACHER'S WORD BANK
The teacher provides a list of words that relate to the text or topic before reading. The meaning could be discussed in advance, or decoded by pupils during the reading of the text and meanings later shared as a class.

15. **Book review**

What you need: books
Subject links: literacy

✦ Pupils write book reviews of their chosen text. These could be laminated and placed inside the book as a book mark for that text. Ensure that the font size and word count are appropriate for the size for the book. If possible, include the reviews on a book section of the school website.

16. Character grids

What you need: rulers to draw grids
Subject links: literacy, RE, history, speaking and listening

Children could use grids to communicate their knowledge and opinions of a character:

✦   CHARACTER GRAPH
   Label the x axis chronologically according to time, chapters or events. Label the y axis with a criteria (level of excitement, wealth, or other criteria for a given character).

✦   RELATIONSHIP CELLS
   List all the characters along both the x and y axis. Each cell should be completed with some detail describing the relationship that they have with each other, including with themselves.

Character graph for Sam

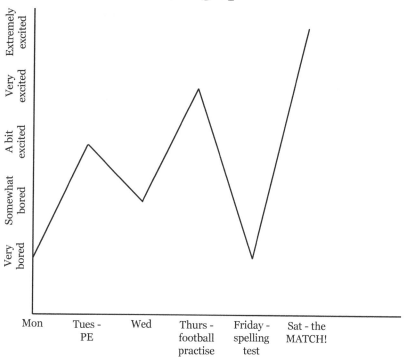

17. **Character work**

What you need: good awareness of characters studied
Subject links: literacy

✦ CHARACTER PROFILE
Create 'Top Trumps®' style cards for characters in a story, detailing statistics, strengths, weaknesses, etc. Make an inventory: compile a list of all the interesting things that they own and use. Draw a map or write a description of the character's bedroom in their own home.

✦ INTERVIEWS
Write interviews in the style of a publication (eg, Hello! Magazine, or The Times), or in the style of a TV or radio broadcast.

✦ LEAGUE TABLES
Rank the characters in league tables using criteria such as morality, wealth, size, etc. Discuss with the class if different ranking criteria produce different results. Ensure all compiled lists include all characters from greatest to least for any given criteria.

✦ QUOTE LABELLED PICTURE
Pupils sketch or draw a character, setting or device that they then label using direct quotes from the text.

✦ RELATIONSHIP WEB
Draw and link different characters with evidence from the text to illustrate their relationship.

✦ THOUGHT BUBBLES
Write what the characters are really thinking in between their spoken dialogue.

18. **Inspiring creative writing**

What you need: For Hero Factory, www.cpherofactory.com. For Mad Machines, access to images of Rube Goldberg or Heath Robinson machines. For Retelling Old Tales, a copy of traditional tales. For Sketch First, paper and pencil. For Toy or Model Adventure, child's own toy or model.
Subject links: literacy

✦ HERO FACTORY
For an inspiring start to creative writing, pupils could visit www.cpherofactory.com to create their own hero, with their own printable comic cover. Even without the web link, pupils may still create a character in the superhero genre, deciding on their character's background, special powers and purpose.

✦ MAD MACHINES
Descriptive and explanatory writing can be supported with these amazing contraptions of engineering by Edwardian inventors Rube Goldberg and Heath Robinson. Simple household tasks are resolved using humorous and excessive designs. They are difficult to visualize, so visit www.rubegoldberg.com. (There are no quality Heath Robinson sites readily available due to copyright issues.) Pupils can first describe the stages involved in operating each contraption, then discuss the merits of such an enterprise.

✦ A fun extension could be the creation of their own Rube Goldberg machine for a simple school or household task.

✦ RETELLING OLD TALES
Pupils select and then retell their own variation of a classic story, such as a fairy tale. Whilst following the original opening and characters, pupils should be free to create their own new, possibly comic, interpretations.

✦ SKETCH FIRST
Sketch the character you are going to describe. This helps pupils visualize and remember to include details that may otherwise be overlooked in writing. Sketches could also be done of relevant tools, machines, creatures or settings. Ensure pupils sketch in pencil only, without colouring, to encourage them to see the activity primarily as a spring board towards more detailed writing. Provide a time limit, maybe five minutes, to maintain momentum and avoid procrastination.

✦ TOY OR MODEL ADVENTURE
Pupils write an adventure based upon a toy or model they may be allowed to bring into school. Pupils could introduce other pupils' toys or models as additional characters to interact with their own.

19. **Information book sections**

What you need: access to accurate information (encyclopedia/Internet)
Subject links: literacy

✦ Divide the class into teams and have each team write a detailed information book about a chosen topic. For example, 'Motorized Transport' could contain sections on motorbikes, sports cars, 4 x 4s, emergency vehicles, etc. Pupils could each write sections individually or in pairs. Emphasize the importance of providing high-quality work from all group members.

✦ Increase the visual appeal by permitting the use of bullet points and accurately labelled illustrations that are printed rather than drawn to ensure the focus remains on literacy rather than art. Pupils should take responsibility for their own investigation and agree a target range for the number of words per page to prevent a lack of written effort or a glut of information. Place emphasis upon third person and precise, detailed writing of informative texts.

20. Reports and reviews

What you need: for Film/Game/TV/Track Review, use website containing media to review film preview, trailer, etc. For Newspaper Reports, examples of newspaper front pages (scanned onto whiteboard or copied as examples). For Sports Reviews, sports event to view (preferably live), cameras (preferably digital), dictaphones, notepads. Subject links: literacy, geography, RE, PE, ICT

✦   FILM/GAME/TV/TRACK REVIEW
Ensuring all media reviewed is age appropriate, view a media clip and review together, modelling the review process on the media used. Once pupils are confident of the skills and format required, they could also review other media with which they are already familiar. Again ensure content is appropriate for the age range.

✦   NEWSPAPER REPORTS
Write a report on a topic studied in a third-person journalistic style. Pictures could be drawn, downloaded or taken using a digital camera. Include modelled details, such as headlines, subheadings, possible alliteration, etc.

✦   SPORTS REVIEWS
Let pupils watch a sports event. They may participate as players, reporters or photographers. Then in groups they combine their roles to produce newspaper articles of the event for rival newspapers. If playing against a team from a different school, e-mail the finished articles to them for pre-arranged feedback. It may be possible for the other school to produce the same work if they are in the same year and compare coverage by the various journalist teams.

21. Newspaper headline: sort and match

What you need: articles either online/paper copy
Subject links: literacy

✦   Provide pupils with a set of headlines and either opening paragraphs or whole articles that have been separated, to match together.

✦   Pupils could then write a new headline for the article and/or a new opening paragraph or article to accompany an existing headline.

22. Newspaper/web news comparison

What you need: articles either online/paper copy
Subject links: literacy

✦   Compare articles about the same story. Focus upon the differences between the articles:
- ❑   Proportion of text/pictures
- ❑   Type/difficulty of vocabulary
- ❑   Obvious bias/point of view
- ❑   Location of story (front page or buried elsewhere)
- ❑   Online/traditional format differences

23. Comparative news

What you need: examples of identical news story in different styles: teletext, TV, radio, newspapers, websites, etc
Subject links: literacy

✦ Using an existing or fictitious news item, place pupils in news teams to produce the same information in the style or layout appropriate for the following formats: teletext, radio, newspapers (broadsheet and tabloid) and news websites.

✦ Each team should discuss and plan how to make the style authentic for each format. They may then decide for themselves, or be directed, as to whether they use a group writing strategy or assign individuals or pairs to produce separately formatted articles.

24. Film education

What you need: www.filmeducation.org, www.bfi.org.uk/education
Subject links: literacy

✦ Use the above links to consider which film to use, timings for relevant slices of the film and how to use the film in the curriculum:
- ❏ Watch the film in small slices. Pupils discuss each slice and then write a simple text, sequence by sequence. Include characterization, emotions, setting, etc.
- ❏ Video a PE or drama lesson or an assembly. Use as a resource to model and discuss successful modelling and information.
- ❏ Use stills to create sequencing, captions, writing frames and storyboards.

25. **Media and plays**
What you need: web video or DVD
Subject links: literacy

✦ Review key scenes from a film and analyse the script, imagery, use of colour, soundtrack, pace, dialogue, lighting, camera angles, etc. Compare and contrast these key elements from each scene.

✦ Create word banks to describe and comment on the scenes in the film.

26. **Ticket design**
What you need: collection of various tickets
Subject links: literacy

✦ Examine a variety of tickets and discuss their purposes. Display the tickets on an interactive whiteboard or provide each group with copies of tickets to enable pupils to examine the tickets together for details. What information is displayed and for what purpose? What format and layout is used and why?

✦ Pupils could then create their own ticket, possibly as part of a story (eg winning ticket from Charlie and the Chocolate Factory, orbital flight with Virgin Galactic, etc).

27. **Posters**

What you need: information related to topic, examples of posters
Subject links: literacy, art, history, geography, RE, MFL

✦ PERSUASIVE POSTERS
Write a persuasive poster or information leaflet about a topic, eg Roman army recruitment drive, applying to join Scott of Antarctica, healthy eating, benefits of exercise, visit a location.

✦ PROPAGANDA POSTERS
Study examples of propaganda posters and discuss the use of imagery, language, colour, setting, lighting and emotion. Pupils then create an appropriate poster for a purpose linked to the topic studied. Ensure specific purpose and target audience are clearly understood with the above details incorporated into a plan prior to sketching.

28.   **Picture that!**

What you need: page containing part of a picture or an artefact, paper, pencils, books
or Internet for research
Subject links: literacy, art, history, geography, RE

✦   FINISH THE PICTURE
      Provide each pupil with a page containing an image that does
      not dominate the picture, but acts as a contextual prompt for
      the event or location that the picture describes or where it is
      set. Pupils then complete the picture as a sketch proving as
      much detail as possible. They should aim to include artefacts,
      costume, landscape and other details appropriate to the
      context.

✦   VISUAL ENQUIRY
      Provide a group with a picture or photograph in the centre
      of a page, and encourage higher order discussion based
      upon what they can see. They may record questions they
      wish answered around the picture, together with ideas as to
      where the answers may be acquired. If some answers may be
      gained from investigating the same resources, individuals or
      pairs within the group could be assigned to feedback answers
      to the group from their research. Ensure that sufficient
      appealing text resources are available if Internet access is
      limited.

29. **Show me**

What you need: pupils' whiteboards, letter fans
Subject links: literacy

Use simple whole-class activities so all can participate simultaneously.

✦   Mini-whiteboards: each pupil uses his/her own whiteboard and pen to 'Think, write and show me', eg use of prefixes, completing a sum, punctuating a sentence, correct spellings.

✦   Letter fans: Used in a similar way to number fans, letter fans can be used for CVC words, abbreviations, prefixes and suffixes, etc.

30. **Role-playing**

What you need: camera. For Homemade Big Book, large 'scrap' book.
Subject links: speaking and listening, literacy, history, geography, RE, PSHE, MFL

✦   ROLE-PLAY
Enact a 30 second section of an extract from a poem, religious text, account of a historical event, etc. For longer extracts divide the text into chunks, allocating a chronological part to each team.

✦   Groups should be arranged in a large circle so everyone can clearly see each other. Each role-play could flow from one to the other aiming to recount a seamless rendition.

✦   HOMEMADE BIG BOOK
Using props and costume, if possible, retell a story or event in role-play. Let pupils take a series of digital photographs that are used to sequence the story. Pupils then collaboratively determine and write the sentences that accompany each picture. Depending upon the number of cameras available, each table or group could prepare, draft, act, photograph, discuss and write their own big book.

31. **Giving instructions**

What you need: For Daily Instructions and Vowel-less Instructions, writing resources or computer and printer. For Model Making Instructions, models or materials to create models.
Subject links: literacy

✦ DAILY INSTRUCTIONS
Rather than the teacher spending considerable time preparing instruction prompts for the class wall, pupils could complete this task. They could also create similar prompts for energy saving, switching off computers properly, healthy eating, locations of sports equipment in the PE cupboard, school maps, directions, room signs, etc.

✦ Emphasize the need for accuracy, first impressions for visitors, as well as the consequences for others of unclear or inaccurate instructions.

✦ MODEL MAKING INSTRUCTIONS
Considering the ongoing popularity of modelling (eg Games Workshop), engage pupils' interest by writing instructions for model making. Then follow the step-by-step instructions for making and displaying the models. If modelling seems too complex, keep it as a link to DT projects on modelling, or to simple tasks such as making paper boats or aeroplanes.

✦ VOWEL-LESS INSTRUCTIONS
In order to gain pupils' attention for an independent task, write the instructions upon the whiteboard, intentionally missing out all the vowels in the writing. This will force pupils to focus and decode what they need to do.

32. **Digital storyboard**
What you need: digital cameras
Subject links: literacy, any

✦ Use digital cameras to produce a storyboard. This could be used to retell or explain any event or process, eg instructions for sports, skills or modelling, ceremonies, historical events (acted out in costume), etc.

33. **Hyperlink PowerPoint**
What you need: access to PowerPoint, information about story
Subject links: literacy, ICT

✦ Use either a factual or story text with PowerPoint. Hyperlinks refer to the clickable connections that take you from one page to another.

✦ For factual texts treat each page as a separate subtopic within the text. When a relevant link is appropriate, show pupils how to embed the link to make a relevant connection to another page within the PowerPoint presentation.

✦ For a story approach, follow the format popular with adventure books where the reader makes a decision or chooses a destination and then turns to the relevant page. In the same way as with factual texts, link a dozen or so 'locations' or options as a character explores a location or resolves a dilemma.

34. **Different perspectives**

What you need: class texts
Subject links: literacy

✦ GENRE EXCHANGE
Pupils transpose a piece of writing in one style into that of a different genre, eg witness statement into a newspaper report.

✦ PROBABILITY CHART
Rank important scenes or pages according to the likelihood of truth or probability, eg most probable to least probable.

✦ STORY COMPARISON CHART
Read out alternative endings or story lines and compile a parallel chronological chart comparing the different versions.

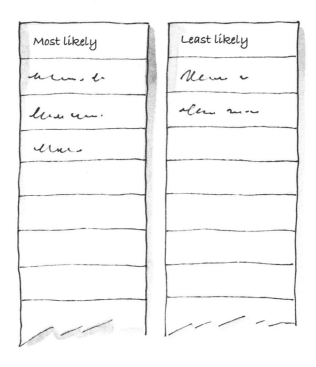

Numeracy

35. Play your cards right

What you need: display cards with values one side, blank other side
Subject links: numeracy

✦　　Support the study of probability and numerical values by playing this game. Teams turn over cards to reveal values, and have to estimate if the next revealed card in a sequence is likely to be higher or lower within a range than the preceding card. Suitable for place value, fractions, decimals ratio, etc.

36. Co-ordinates symmetrical mask

What you need: squared paper, colour pens, scissors
Subject links: numeracy, DT

✦　　Pupils create masks (possibly with linked topic theme) that are drawn using written co-ordinates and a line of symmetry using an x/y axis grid.

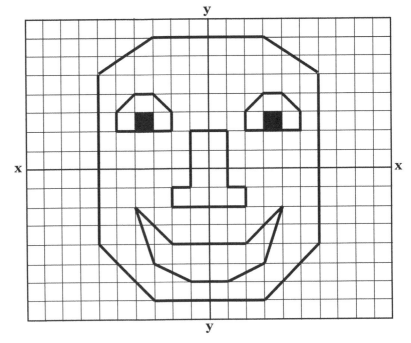

37. **Digital root patterns**

What you need: squared paper
Subject links: numeracy, art

✦ List a times table and add together the digits that make up the answers, for example:

6 times table	Add	Digital root
6	0 + 6	6
12	1 + 2	3
18	1 + 8	9
24	2 + 4	6
30	3 + 0	3
36	3 + 6	9, etc

✦ Use this 6, 3, 9 digital root to produce a linear pattern. For example, draw a line 6 squares long, then turn left 90 degrees and draw the next line for 3 squares, turn left at 90 degrees and now draw 9 squares etc. Continue this pattern until you return to the original starting point. Compare the different patterns produced by different digital roots.

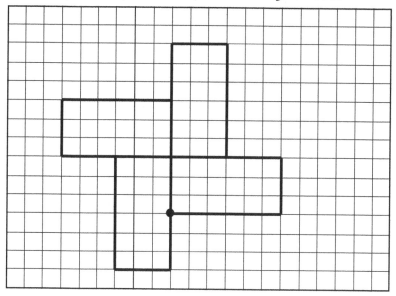

38. **Times tables graphs**
What you need: graph paper, Cuisenaire® rods (optional)
Subject links: numeracy

✦ Pupils produce a bar chart for the times tables they are currently learning so they can visualize the rate of increase in the multiples answer.

✦ Alternatively Cuisenaire® rods could be laid down upon a labelled axis. The x axis should detail the multipliers and the y axis the answers to be read off the graph.

39. **Roman times tables**
What you need: grid for 10 x 10 times tables
Subject links: numeracy, history

✦ Create a grid for pupils to complete a multiplication 100 square of all their times tables. Pupils should use Roman numerals to fill in the blank 100 squares.

X	I	II	III	IV	V	VI	VII	VIII	IX	X
I	I	II	III	IV	V	VI	VII	VIII	IX	X
II	II	IV	VI	VIII	X	XII	XIV	XVI	XVIII	XX
III	III	VI	IX	XII	XV	XVIII	XXI	XXIV	XXVII	XXX
IV	IV	VIII	XII	XVI	XX	XXIV	XXVIII	XXXII	XXXVI	XL
V	V	X	XV	XX	XXV	XXX	XXXV	XL	XLV	L
VI	VI	XII	XVIII	XXIV	XXX	XXXVI	XLII	XLVIII	LIV	LX
VII	VII	XIV	XXI	XXVIII	XXXV	XLII	XLIX	LVI	LXIII	LXX
VIII	VIII	XVI	XXIV	XXXII	XL	XLVIII	LVI	LXIV	LXXII	LXXX
IX	IX	XVIII	XXVII	XXXVI	XLV	LIV	LXIII	LXXII	LXXXI	XC
X	X	XX	XXX	XL	L	LX	LXX	LXXX	XC	C

40. **Ancient Egyptian multiplication**

What you need: nothing
Subject links: numeracy, history

✦ To calculate more complex sums the ancient Egyptians often used adding and doubling to answer multiplication queries, for example:

18 x 12

✦ Work using 2 columns. In the first show the numbers of 12s worked out and in the second column show the amount that they would produce, eg:

1 x 12 =	12

✦ Now begin to double:

2 x 12 =	24

✦ Continue this process until you are using numbers just below the multiplier used in the original question (in this case 18).

4 x 12 =	48
8 x 12 =	96
16 x 12 =	192

✦ There would be no purpose in multiplying any higher since that would be greater than the answers needed.

✦ To make 18 x 12 you need to work out what to add to 16 to make 18 (ie 2). Add together 16 x 12 and 2 x 12:

16 x 12 =	192
2 x 12 =	24
18 x 12 =	216

Science

41. Line graph narrative

What you need: line graph
Subject links: science, literacy

✦ Use a line graph to provide a context for a narrative or explanation text describing the process unfolding and recorded by the graph.

✦ Reluctant writers may be enthused enough by practical science to be willing to write. For example, use personification to describe their experiences as a water droplet: starting as a cool swimming liquid molecule, to heating, boiling and evaporating as airborn gas before cooling, condensing and skydiving as falling liquid.

42. Recount

What you need: experience of practical science or PE
Subject links: science, PE, literacy

✦ Experience a practical science or PE lesson. Pupils then provide a detailed, accurate recount of what was accomplished and why. Ensure the inclusion of correct techniques and conclusions.

History

43. **History pictorial activities**

What you need: paper, pencils, rulers, optional colours, examples of suitable comic strips, topic knowledge

Subject links: history, RE, literacy, geography, MFL, PSHE, art

✦ COMIC STRIP
Pupils retell an event, story, era or location visually using a comic strip format. View some scanned or copied examples of comic strips. Focus upon detail within the pictures, and the way a comic strip recounts a story. Draw attention to the way text is included within speech and thought bubbles.

✦ Initially produce a paper sketch only, moving onwards to black and white ink, before adding colour. Emphasize as much accurate visual information as possible, eg costume, landscape, design, wildlife and phrases/sayings.

✦ LOGOS OF THE GODS
The vast number of pagan Gods in historical cultures can be confusing. Pupils can create a simple logo for each God to help remember their specific power and role in their culture. You could also apply this to kings, queens and other rulers. For example: bolt of lightning for Thor, chariot for Boudicca, etc.

✦ MENU
Create and draw a menu for the culture or characters (real or fictitious) studied. As an extension, pupils could add their own comments on the healthiness of the meal and their own preferences or why a character or real people studied might enjoy their suggestions.

✦ MEANS OF TRANSPORT
Illustrate and label the means of transport utilized by peoples
within the culture being studied depending upon status,
region and purpose. The following categories may help: river,
seas, rich, poor, trade, military, pilgrim, farmer, explorer,
nobility, royalty.

44. **Historical maps**

What you need: topic knowledge, visual prompts, local maps
Subject links: history, art

✦ HISTORICAL PICTURE MAP
Draw a town picture map, showing important buildings,
farm crops, entertainment venues, palaces, places of worship,
military sites, schools, etc. In individual buildings (especially
homes) focus upon the detail of furnishings and utensils
instead.

✦ PLACE NAMES
Explore the meaning of place names in the vicinity. Use
district and village names since these tend to be older and
more authentic. Many estates often have themed as opposed
to historic names. It may be useful to develop a root word
bank which could also be used as part of a display.

45. House comparison

What you need: topic knowledge or source material
Subject links: history, geography

✦ FLOOR PLAN
Draw a floor plan showing the size and scale of a building or a room in a property. Compare rooms and buildings by income, ethnicity, rural/urban, etc. Include possible locations of furniture appropriate for cultures and social groups studied.

✦ COMPARISON CHART
Compare two or more contrasting features of properties within a chart: building materials, furniture, locations, fuel and heating, light, water, shelter from the elements, smoke, animals, etc.

✦ COLOUR LABELLED SKETCH
Draw and clearly label interiors of two properties using the same scale if possible. Use realistic colours and artefacts as guides.

46. Rich/poor comparison chart

What you need: topic knowledge, topic books
Subject links: history, geography

✦ Create a comparison chart showing the contrasting experiences of rich and poor within the context studied. Features could include water, food, housing, clothing, health, belongings, leisure.

47. TV news

What you need: desk and chair at front, optional camcorder, optional visual aids relevant to news story
Subject links: history, RE, geography, speaking and listening, PSHE, MFL, ICT

✦ Pupils prepare and deliver a newscast regarding an event or human interest story being studied. They could report on 'current' news such as Viking raids, Biblical events, scenes from a book (eg Charlie winning the golden ticket to the chocolate factory). Emphasize mature delivery in the style of newscasting and interviewing techniques.

✦ ICT pupils could edit their own video footage and include reference to maps and charts in the style of a news channel.

48. When they were young

What you need: existing topic/character knowledge, relevant texts (auto/biographies)
Subject links: history, RE, literacy, geography

✦ Write about or draw and illustrate a famous character from a different time or location, when he/she was the same age as the pupils. Include clothing, hobbies, schooling, lifestyle, beliefs, age of working life, etc.

✦ This activity could be used to illustrate historical changes, geographical and cultural differences, or to build an understanding of a character and why he/she acts in a certain manner.

49. Personal and class timelines

What you need: paper and colour pens
Subject links: history, numeracy

✦   Pupils produce their own timeline of their life from birth to the present. A simpler version, which could be tried first to help them learn how to space events appropriately and consecutively, would be a simple timeline of the day from waking up to the present lesson.

✦   At the end of the year, extend a personal timeline into a class one. Celebrate all the topics, trips and events of the year with a timeline, recording the key events of the past 12 months. Pupils could decorate the timeline as they choose as part of the celebration of their success.

50. Historical timetable

What you need: topic knowledge
Subject links: history, numeracy

✦   Create a historical timetable, detailing times spent completing tasks in a typical day from the era being studied. Include the whole day from waking through to going to sleep.

51. **Alphabets**

What you need: copy of foreign/historic alphabet and link to our own alphabet
Subject links: history, geography, RE

✦ Pupils write messages or official documents using appropriate vocabulary, or create artefacts (scrolls, model tombs, wax tablets, etc) utilizing hieroglyphs, runes or any other alphabet. Hold competitions to decode cryptic messages in the fastest time.

52. **Scribe a letter**

What you need: awareness of character studied
Subject links: history, literacy, RE

✦ Acting in character, pupils could write a letter in character. The letter should be for a specific purpose. For example: Henry VIII ordering an execution and stating why; Moses writing to Pharaoh; Willie Wonka writing to Charlie, etc. Afterwards pupils can evaluate how well the letter achieves the purpose for which it is written.

Geography

53. **Local or world/national picture maps**

What you need: pictures or labels of buildings or geographical features, map outline of local area drawn on board, world/national map, Blu-tac®
Subject links: geography, history

✦   Decide whether to use a local or world/national map. Using the board to model, pupils explain the map and how it works (main features, compass points, etc). Using pictures or labels of local features (park, post office, church, etc) for a local map, or geographical features (mountain ranges, seas, big cities, etc) for a world/national map, pupils fasten them to the board in the correct location.

✦   This could easily be turned into a race with points scored for accuracy with small teams competing to a set time scale. Differentiation could easily be accommodated by providing harder items to be located and labelled for some teams.

✦   For history, compare the location of older and newer buildings, cities or civilizations on the map.

54.   **Virtual maps**

What you need: www.360cities.net, Google Earth or similar, tracing paper
Subject links: literacy, geography

✦   LOCAL GOOGLE MAPS
        Using a model on the whiteboard, trace over an aerial
        shot of Google maps. Let pupils identify the school and
        surrounding features, then label them either on a trace or an
        unlabelled print-off. Change the view on Google to display
        road names to confirm accuracy. If printing off the road map
        only, pupils could colour code land use.

✦   If studying a geographical or historical location, consider
        looking at a Google overview of Hadrian's Wall, Sea of
        Galilee, Beijing, etc. Google Schools (www.google.co.uk/intl/
        em/school) names major features of many key cities.

✦   VIRTUAL EXPLORATION
        Use highly visual websites and tools like those above to
        explore an environment together either through the whole
        class looking at the whiteboard or individual laptops. Discuss
        what can be seen and decoded from the images: events,
        purpose, materials, life, time of day, location, etc. Use as a
        discussion or writing start point.

55. **Sports map**

What you need: atlases, Internet access, travel brochures
Subject links: geography

✦ Use an international sports event that is topical and available to follow easily by pupils at home. Pupils can then be given a country to study that is competing in the event, possibly forming their own teams if there are more pupils than nations participating. They can then investigate the nation concerned (geography, population size, wildlife, etc).

✦ You could also suggest finding a non-air route for people to travel to reach the sports grounds from the participating nation, including time zones and km distance.

56. **Task map**

What you need: local or school maps
Subject links: geography

✦ Create a map for a specific purpose, eg the fastest or shortest route to a location such as a class trip or local feature.

✦ Alternatively, use a school or classroom map to show how to move most efficiently to perform a task.

57. **Choropleth map**

What you need: access to Google maps, print-offs, tracing paper
Subject links: geography

✦ A choropleth map type shows areas with the same features or numerical value. For example, if discovering the distribution of shops in a central area, or flowers in a meadow, divide the area studied into equal sized grids. Record each studied object with a cross. Write the number of crosses in the grid. In a true choropleth map the same colour is used at different shades, with darker shades indicating higher values. The children's age (or the limitation of resources) may determine if different colours should be used instead. Shade each grid square and make an appropriate key to record the range.

✦ Pupils should then explore why they think certain patterns are discovered. For example, if multiple choropleth maps are made of more than one type of object in the same area, do we see identical or contrasting patterns?

58. **Identifying key features**

What you need: pictures, maps or photographs (1 per child), tracing paper, pens
Subject links: geography, science, RE, PSHE, speaking and listening, history, art, DT

✦   Provide pupils with a picture, map or photograph and let them identify its key features. Use clear plastic, acetate or tracing paper to trace these main features, then label and provide a title. This exercise could be used for most subjects, eg the human body, street historical scene or ceremony, etc.

✦   Pupils then exchange completed traced sheets for comparisons on identified key features, discussing why they chose as they did and why they believe certain features are key. The teacher could model pupils' work on acetate on an OHP, overlaying the original image.

59. **Photo record**

What you need: digital cameras
Subject links: geography, science

✦   Pupils use a digital camera to plan and take photographs of a locality in order to record and illustrate its key features. They must be able to explain why they selected their objects, angles and viewpoints, considering changes in a location during different times of the day, as well as the roles of people and their places in the local environment.

60. **Holiday destinations**

What you need: atlases, pencils, paper, tourist brochures
Subject links: geography

✦   HOLIDAY MAPS
Pupils locate a country where they have already been or would like to visit. They then draw an outline map of that country recording its main features (capital cities, major mountains, etc), and routes or locations that they would visit there.

✦   SELLING TOURISM
Create a travel leaflet informing visitors of the sites and features of interest to see and experience in a location taken from a studied text.

61. Estate agent

What you need: reference texts, images of appropriate building
Subject links: history, literacy, geography

✦ Play the role of an estate agent, by creating an advertisement for the sale of a property from a topic or text studied. Use appropriate historical or geographical terms for the rooms, materials, décor, furnishings, location, etc. This could apply to novels (hobbit holes, ginger bread houses, etc) as well as to real world examples.

62. Cloud survey

What you need: display materials
Subject links: geography, art

✦ Visit the following site for some excellent free downloads on cloud types identification:
http://science-edu.larc.nasa.gov/SCOOL/cldchart.html

✦ Survey and identify clouds, and create a tick sheet to spot clouds over a time frame, maybe one or two weeks.

✦ To show the different cloud types, create a display using photos, cotton wool and other materials illustrating the altitude and size in miles or km of clouds. Contrast with heights of mountains. This could be used as a cross-curricular idea, using chalks or pastels on blue card to draw clouds. Label the clouds with adjectives to help identify the type.

63. **Micro water cycle**

What you need: very hot water, marble, large container, a heavy or weighted smaller container, and cling film
Subject links: geography, science

✦ Recreate a water cycle using: very hot water, marble, a large container, a heavy or weighted smaller container, and cling film.

✦ Place the smaller, heavy container inside the larger one and pour the hot water around it (not in it). Cover the large container top with cling film. Place the marble on the cling film over the smaller container so that any condensation will drip into it. Pupils will see evaporation from the hot water and condensation on the underside of the cling film.

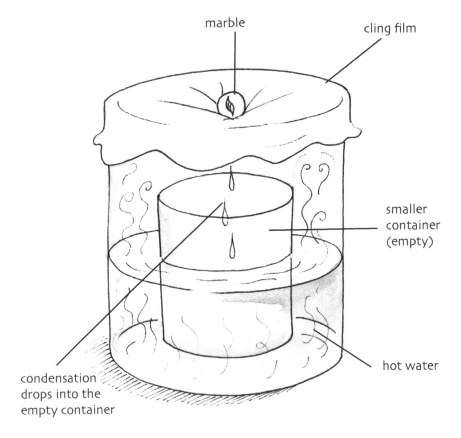

marble

cling film

smaller container (empty)

hot water

condensation drops into the empty container

64.   Global food

What you need: access to home food cupboards, worksheet to record food type and country of origin
Subject links: geography, numeracy

✦   Pupils record the food type and country of origin of products in their food cupboards at home. They then plot this on a world map in school to show the globalization of their food supply.

✦   Extension: calculate the cumulative food miles travelled for the recorded food products.

MFL

65.   Symbol and word match cards

What you need: blank or prepared paired cards, timers
Subject links: MFL, numeracy, history, geography, music, PSHE, RE

✦   This is a paired card game that could be produced by pairs of pupils themselves. Sketch or write a symbol, word or objective on a card and write the translation in the MFL on a different card. Create themed packs for the same topic. Pupils compete to see who can match all the cards in the fastest time.

✦   The cards may be used to play snap or a traditional matching pairs game where all cards are initially located face down on desk and turned over two at a time by each player. If the pair matches, the player gets to keep the cads and has another go. The player with the most pairs at the end wins.

✦   These card games are also useful when teaching classification and matching equivalent sums.

66. **Body and clothes beetle drive**

What you need: dice, pens, paper
Subject links: MFL

✦ Played in the same manner as beetle drive, small groups of pupils sit around a table and take it in turns to roll a dice. The six numbers can be allocated to a body part, facial feature or item of clothing which must be drawn when the specific number is rolled.

✦ For older more advanced pupils why not allocate the first rolls to the body, then when complete, the same number could refer to facial features and finally, to dressing the character. It may be helpful to display the MFL term and dice number, either on the board or on a worksheet. Pupils must state the name of the body part correctly to add it to the sheet.

RE

67. **Prayer**

What you need: paper, colouring pencils or pens
Subject links: RE, art

✦ Draw a prayer – NOT a picture of people praying but the picture as a prayer in itself.

✦ Variations could include spider charts to show the good things in life for which we are grateful, or a map prayer showing the locations of people, objects, places and hobbies for which we are thankful.

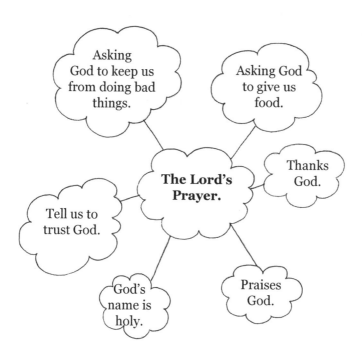

PSHE

68. Action

What you need: paper, pens, Blu-tac®, whiteboard
Subject links: PSHE, RE, ICT

✦ Pupils suggest class rules based upon positive behaviour and expectations. Hold a race for five minutes for team pairs to write down as many as they can think of.

✦ Share results with the class. Accepted (possibly voted for) ideas should be written on the whiteboard. Avoid duplication but add detail if appropriate. Try to condense to a few workable rules and gain class vote or agreement to abide by them.

✦ Highlight one rule a day by clearly displaying it in the classroom as a shared goal. Pupils could mime or act out a mini sketch illustrating an example of applying this rule.

✦ Improve ICT keyboard skills and produce a PowerPoint presentation of the agreed rules with appropriate video clips, graphics, symbolic colours, etc.

69. **Role models**

What you need: Internet access, display board
Subject links: PSHE, ICT

✦ Using Google images, or similar, find pictures of suitable role models chosen by pupils.

✦ Pupils should discuss why they admire these people and how they achieved their successes. Draw out the hard work, planning, education and training they undertook to achieve them.

✦ Make a display using pictures of role models side-by-side those of pupils, with speech or thought bubbles coming from pupils stating what they will do to achieve their aims.

✦ Kinaesthetic link: Pupil could mime/role-play their role model. The rest of the class needs to guess who it is and explain WHY and HOW he/she achieved his/her potential.

✦ Ensure the emphasis remains upon the hard work and sacrifice put into obtaining their success. Point out where pupils are already following in their footsteps, as well as what they could do to achieve more in the future.

70. Positive words
What you need: positive words on cards, pens
Subject links: PSHE, RE

✦ Use a set of cards with a positive word or value written on each one. Provide one for every pupil. Alternatively ask the pupils to create a list that could be written on the board. Ensure that each word is understood by asking pupils to describe what uncertain words may mean.

✦ A word card is given to each pupil who then has to decide which pupil(s) best match the quality of that word. Ensure that each pupil may only be picked once. Ideally the teacher should retain a few words for themselves to nominate anyone missed by the rest of the class.

71. Personal timetable
What you need: graph paper/computer to create timetable
Subject links: PSHE, maths, RE, ICT, history

✦ Pupils draw a whole week of 24 hour days to evaluate how they spend their time. Compare sleeping times, hobbies, amount of exercise, means of transport, healthy/sustainable living, religious lives of various faith groups. Spreadsheets could be used to colour code information and present weekly totals or daily comparisons in graphic form.

72. **Visual healthy menu**

What you need: prior awareness of healthy eating
Subject links: PSHE, DT, science

✦ Provide blank circle 'dinner plates' on which pupils draw the food they think comprises a healthy meal. This could be expanded to plan healthy lunches for a school dinner week or more, encompassing seasonal and local produce. The planning could also be expanded to include lunches, evening dinners and healthy snacks.

73. **Lifestyle map**

What you need: pencils, rulers, colour pencils
Subject links: geography, PSHE, numeracy

✦ Pupils draw a sketch map of the locations of activities from their own life. Starting with their main home in the centre they draw other locations, (school, family, swimming baths, etc) further or closer to the home based upon the perceived distance and travel time to each place.

✦ The map should resemble a spider diagram. Add thickness to the connecting lines to show the number of times that journey is completed each month or the level of importance the child attaches to that place. These distance and travel time lines could be colour coded to show healthy choices (cycling/walking) or other modes of transport.

General

74. Mime

What you need: nothing
Subject links: any, speaking and listening, literacy

✦   Instead of role-play, use this silent version. Mime can be used to identify verbs, adjectives, characters, historic/religious tasks, etc.

✦   A variation includes freeze framing during a particular sequence, or simply presenting a still scene using frozen action/facial expression to communicate ideas.

✦   To create a magic mime, read out a text and indicate with a magic wand that pupils should mime to the text. The magic wand could be used to indicate when to begin and end the specific section of the text that should be mimed. This encourages active listening as pupils listen to gather clues from the spoken text.

75. Instructions

What you need: nothing
Subject links: any

✦ Pupils work in pairs to provide instructions that show how to complete a historical, religious or cultural task, for example throwing a javelin or making a cup of tea. Pupils should act or mime each stage to see if the instructions are accurate and include all necessary details.

✦ The class acts out a task only as instructed. This highlights any missing or unclear instructions. Make group suggestions for improving the instructions so that the individual authors can make the changes needed.

✦ Optionally, these improved instructions could then be passed onto another class for evaluation by following the instructions themselves and commenting upon their effectiveness as feedback to the original children.

76. Thought lines

What you need: nothing
Subject links: literacy, science, RE, PSHE, speaking and listening, history, geography

✦ Arrange pupils in two equal rows facing one another. Each pupil states a point of view regarding an issue, and they may all speak at the same time. One pupil, acting either as a character from a text or as him/herself, walks down the path between the two rows. When he/she reaches the end, the pupil states with which viewpoint he/she agrees and joins that chosen row. This allows higher order thought and encourages pupils to reason on their own or according to a character's choices.

✦ This could be expanded to include hypothesis in science, choices facing people in other eras or places, as well as ethical decisions.

77. Name game

What you need: optional hand-held name cards, chairs in a circle + one spare
Subject links: speaking and listening

✦ Sit pupils on chairs in a circle. If the group are new to each other, have hand-held name cards, written clearly enough to be seen from the other side of the circle. Leave one chair empty.

✦ The person with the empty chair on their left calls out the name of a person to come and sit beside him/her. Both pupils then swap names and name cards if used.

✦ It is now the turn of the person with the empty chair on his/her left to call out a name. They repeat the process.

✦ The objective is to give other players their original name back when it is your turn to call. They then sit out and withdraw their chair from the circle. Play continues with the player with the empty chair on their left. Continue until there are two final joint winners.

78. Secret whiteboards

What you need: pupil whiteboards and pens
Subject links: PSHE

✦ To encourage totally honest responses that children may wish to share, tell pupils to stand in an inward facing circle. After they write on their boards they hold them the correct way up behind their backs. The teacher may then circulate around the outside of the circle to gauge their true responses.

79. **Getting out of the classroom**

What you need: for Question Trails, hidden question cards, answer sheets, pens, clipboards
Subject links: any

✦   QUESTION TRAILS
Hide a number of questions around a location (hall, playground, classroom, etc). Pupils must locate the numbered questions and answer them in the correct place on the sheet within a given time limit. Differentiate by providing different colours, fonts and symbols of questions for different groups. Each group must answer its own set of questions within a time limit.

✦   Increase the amount of pupil interest by taping question cards to the underside of furniture, inside cupboards, sideways along pillars, etc.

✦   STOP THE CLASS, I WANT TO GET OUT!
If the classroom is stuffy and hot, or if the class is restless, stop fighting their fidgets and get the class outside for a five minute walk around the school building at a brisk pace. Leave the windows wide open while you are out, even if it's a cold day; it will soon warm up upon 30 bodies' return.

80. 3-D Carroll diagrams

What you need: 3-D objects possibly linked to topic, hula hoops, rulers or string to create grids
Subject links: any

✦ The teacher provides a range of objects or artefacts, and determines categories for sorting them, eg religious objects or historical artefacts based on domestic or working use. Objects could also be linked to a character from a text. Alternatively, instead of using objects, use name cards to refer to gods, leaders or places.

✦ Pupils then place the objects or name cards in the correct places on the 3-D Carroll diagrams. Ideally a different activity could take place at each table and the entire class could gather around each table for the correct answers to be revealed.

✦ Extension: Pupils could be given objects, especially 3-D shapes, and challenged to create Carroll diagrams that need to be decoded.

	Greek	Roman
God	Hermes Apollo	Jupiter Pluto
Person		Julius Caesar

Hercules   Mark Anthony

81. Sorting ideas

What you need: hula hoops, word cards or objects, diagram labels, OHP and pens, labelled trays

Subject links: any

✦ KEY WORDS
Circle or underline words upon the whiteboard according to a given criteria, eg adjectives.

✦ TRAY SORT
Place objects or word cards into the correct labelled tray or sequence, eg plants or animals.

✦ VENN SORTING
Use hula hoops to create a simple Venn diagram on the floor. Label and explain the criteria to pupils. Pairs of pupils then place word or number cards or objects into the correct categories. Make this task more competitive by using a timer. Create several different Venn diagrams about the room with pupils rotating from station to station in order to complete them.

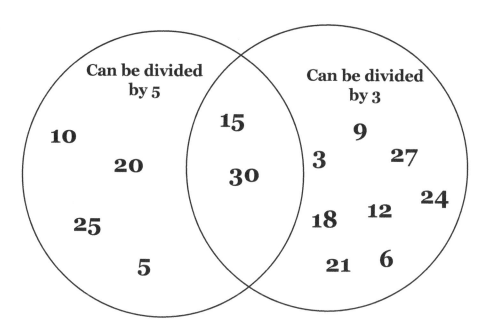

82. **Sequencing**

What you need: prepared sequences on whiteboards or cards ready to be rearranged into correct order
Subject links: literacy, history, PE, RE, geography, PSHE, speaking and listening

✦ Write down either on small whiteboards or on cards the individual stages of a process, eg volcanic explosion, making a salad, the Lord's Prayer, etc.

✦ Pupils stand in a line and hold a sequence card each. They are then rearranged by classmates into the correct order by polite instructions. (This is a good speaking and listening exercise.)

✦ Make a race by forming teams who then compete to get the sequence into the correct order in the shortest possible time.

✦ Pupils can work in pairs to rearrange a sequence from a chopped up paper sheet. The whole class then discuss and confirm the correct order. Pupils can also create and cut out their own sequences which other pupils attempt to solve.

83. **Washing line**

What you need: washing line, pegs, word, number, symbol or picture cards
Subject links: any

✦ This is a variation on sequencing activities. Peg word, number, symbol or picture cards onto a washing line in desired orders, eg definitions of size: micro, tiny, small, medium, large, largest; or fractions. Arrange words into the correct order in a sentence, or numbers and symbols for a sum. Place events or stages in the correct order. Make this task more competitive by setting a time limit.

Literacy

84. **Fun spelling**

What you need: clear display of the whole alphabet and its actions
Subject links: speaking and listening

✦ WAKE UP SPELLING
Display all 26 letters of the alphabet. Allocate a simple body movement to each letter. Four different moves may work best, although you may add more if you wish. Initially start with simple desk bound movements, for example:

A =	Stand up and sit down
B =	Raise left arm
C =	Wiggle your eyebrows
D =	Nod your head

✦ Repeat these patterns for each of the rest of the letters.

✦ Ensure the letters and actions are grouped clearly on the board. This is a very useful activity for removing fidgeting, waking up pupils and enforcing some spelling simultaneously.

✦ FINGER SPELLING
To reinforce correct spellings pupils write the determined word in the air or on their desk with their finger. They can repeat this process with their other hand and also with their eyes shut. Pupils should then visually check their spelling with that written down by the teacher.

85. Tactile words

What you need: physically rough paper, pencils, play dough
Subject links: literacy

✦ Pupils write words using a pencil (not pen) on rough (not smooth) paper. The friction created helps inform muscle memory as pupils write out a required word in a clear size. The pupil then uses 'strings' of play dough to trace over the written word. Tracing over the 'string' word with their fingers, enforces correct letter and word formation and provides the pupil with a tactile experience.

86. Adjective word bank

What you need: objects, paper, optional dictionaries
Subject links: literacy

✦ Have a large number of objects for pupils to touch. Distribute them around the classroom with a piece of paper with each. Pupils investigate the objects and write down a name and an adjective for each. Points could be offered for accurate, original and correctly spelt words.

✦ If many spellings need correcting, have a dictionary race, providing children with the first four letters to maintain pace. Differentiate by offering different spellings to different groups. Display words in a word bank.

87. **Role-play**
What you need: illustration, text
Subject links: literacy, PSHE

✦ MISSING SCENES
Challenge pupils to write, act out or perform an audio play of any scenes that might have taken place within a story but are missed out by the author.

✦ PAST AND FUTURE ROLE-PLAY
Make an illustration visible to the whole class. Discuss with pupils what they can actually observe. Pupils should break into groups, ideally the same number as there are characters in the scene. Begin by deciding what happened to the characters. Pupils can then role-play up to the exact point illustrated. When they reach this point, they briefly freeze before continuing to provide their interpretation as to what happens next.

88. **Student sculpture**
What you need: nothing
Subject links: speaking and listening, PSHE

✦ Divide pupils into pairs. One pupil 'sculpts' the other by moving them into appropriate poses. The other pupil, the 'clay', co-operates fully. This can be used to encourage discussion, or to find alternatives to a scenario involving key characters.

89. **Mr Men™ books**

What you need: card, paper, felt tips
Subject links: literacy, PSHE, art, DT

✦ Have pupils write and illustrate a brand new Mr Men or Little Miss and then take it down to the lower school to read and present to younger children. Take two or three drafts to get it right. Emphasize presentation, spellings and grammar. If produced to a high standard it could be used as a lower school resource.

90. **Book swap circle**

What you need: a book per child
Subject links: literacy

✦ Pupils take their current reading books and sit in small mixed groups (not friendship groups since the idea is exposure to new texts). Each pupil passes their own book to the person on their left. Everyone then reads in silence for three minutes. Pupils then swap and repeat the process until everyone in the group has read each of the other pupils' books for three minutes.

✦ Pupils then discuss each book at a time, commenting on their initial impressions, the cover and title, the story openings, characters, settings and, finally, genre. Did they like what they read? Would they now consider this genre in the future? Why or why not?

91. **Product review**

What you need: access to product review articles: online or paper copies
Subject links: literacy

✦ Pupils write their own product reviews, based on real or fictitious products. Look at product reviews online at www.which.co.uk and www.whatcar.com, both of which offer examples. Many women's and consumer magazines also often contain product reviews. (Which? Online charges £1 for a month's subscription to access their reviews.)

✦ A difficulty with online reviews, however, is that although they can illustrate the written style of a review and can engage the class (review video or photos of the latest £150k sports cars anyone?), they may be removed from pupils' own experiences, limiting their ability to create original feedback. Avoid parroting from a website, and use the online site for modelling purposes only.

✦ Bring food or model toys into school to provide a more hands-on experience. Children can hold and study the food/toys before attempting to write their review.

92. **Model making**

What you need: card, scissors, materials, felts, glue, etc
Subject links: literacy, art, DT

✦ 3-D CHARACTER
Create a simple model of the main character from a story.
Using a card cutout is often the most straightforward way.
If multiple characters are involved, tables or teams of pupils
could create and equip their characters accordingly. Place
some emphasis upon details in order to provide plenty of
background.

✦ Pupils should fill in a background checklist detailing some
element from their character's past, secret, strengths,
weaknesses, preferences, future plans etc. They should try
to include these details in their model. Use the models as a
stimulus to support writing.

✦ MODEL OF SETTING
Make a model of your favourite scene using the descriptions
and details provided in the text.

93. **Investigating characters**

What you need: chosen character pupils may be familiar with
Subject links: literacy, history, RE

✦ WRITTEN INTERVIEW
In pairs pupils both take on the roles of characters from studied texts, deciding between themselves which ones they will be. Both pupils then write a list of interview questions that they will swap with their partner, who will then answer in written form in character.

✦ VERBAL INTERVIEW
This could be done as an auditory exercise using recording equipment. Pupils would be encouraged to use inflection in their voices to assist in developing the interview and character role.

✦ VIPs
Pupils or staff prepare in advance to arrive as a famous character (Pharaoh, Martin Luther King, etc) in costume. Act and talk like the character. The rest of the class question and interview them. Either an adult takes on the role of the famous character, or a pupil from each table. The rest of the table support with props and prompts. One table at a time presents their character to the class.

94. **Lost**

What you need: nothing, although pictures of wild places, compass, torch, map, wood and other things with a jungle feel could all build up the atmosphere (if possible use the outdoor classroom)
Subject links: literacy, geography

✦ Inform pupils their aeroplane has crashed on a remote Pacific island. Your class all survive the crash and form separate teams to explore. What items do you need to take from your luggage scattered on the beach? Create a list of things you would need to survive. Write down all the objects.

✦ What skills will you have to develop to help you survive? List or act out these skills, eg hunting, fishing, building a shelter (young males aspiring to be Ray Mears will love this one), finding water, discovering edible plants, making a fire. Write out instructions for each action and any objects you need to find or make, eg tent, spear, repairing clothes, making a place to sleep, constructing a shelter. Use websites containing video footage of these skills. You can also create diary entries.

✦ With the class, create a random dice roll scenario where each of the 1–6 sides results in a consequence, eg tropical storm, active volcano, etc, that add random dimension to record keeping scenarios.

✦ Allow teams to work together to problem solve in this exercise. Reward team skills, accurate written communication and technical solutions. The winning team could be the one who, through their experiences, produces the best survival manual.

Numeracy

95. **Shape maths**

What you need: number cards, 3 x 3 grid square
Subject links: numeracy

✦ SQUARES – In groups of nine, number the pupils as follows: three number 1s, three number 2s and three number 3s. Within a large 3 x 3 grid square they arrange themselves so that each sum across and down adds up to 6.

✦ With nine pupils numbered 1–9, they arrange themselves in a 3 x 3 grid aiming to ensure that the subtracted differences between adjacent squares is odd. To simplify, do NOT include diagonal links, only those side to side along the edges of the squares.

✦ With eight pupils, use the edges of a square only and not the internal part. Pupils position themselves with a pupil at every corner and a pupil halfway along the middle of the edge of each square. Each pupil is numbered 1–8 and the pupils have to arrange themselves so that the sum of each side is 12.

✦ TRIANGLES – Arrange the class in groups of six and number the pupils as follows: two number 1s, three number 2s and one number 3. The teams race to arrange themselves so that when three pupils stand at the points of the triangle and the other three stand halfway along each side, each side of the triangle adds up to 5.

✦ Repeat the above process but number the pupils 1–6. They need to rearrange themselves so that the sides add up to 9.

✦ LINES – Divide pupils into groups of five. Within each group, number pupils 1–5 standing in a single line. They need to rearrange themselves so that between each number the difference is greater than 1.

96. Team angles

What you need: rope
Subject links: numeracy

✦ In a large space, divide the class into teams. Two pupils in each team are to show a given angle using a rope. To do this, the rest of the team arrange themselves initially into a 180 degree protractor shape, spacing themselves at regular intervals. If there are any D shapes marked on the hall/playground floor, use these. Starting at 0 degrees, the two pupils with the rope indicate a given angle. Repeat for different angles. By the end, pupils should have a better visual idea of what a given angle (to the nearest 15 degrees) looks like.

✦ Further differentiation could be provided by pupils having to identify the angle name. Advanced teams could compete in the same way up to 360 degrees and the less able up to 90 degrees.

97. Shape creation

What you need: paper
Subject links: numeracy

✦ All the class starts with an identical piece of paper. Ask what 2-D shape it is. Challenge them to create specific 2-D shapes, eg square, right angled triangle, irregular pentagon, hexagons, octagons, etc, using folds only.

98. Kinaesthetic patterns

What you need: any resource to make patterns, sports cones, balls, coloured leaves, toys, etc
Subject links: numeracy

✦ Create patterns and sequences using physical objects rather than paper-based work. Many topic linked resources could be made into sequences (eg light bulbs, buzzers, switches, etc, plant leaf types or mammal, reptile, etc).

✦ Encourage higher order thinking by encouraging less obvious patterns (carnivore, herbivore, omnivore, etc) rather than a mere standard size, shape or colour.

99. Times table stand up factors

What you need: large cards with the numbers 3–12 written on them
Subject links: numeracy

✦ Each pupil holds up a card with a number from 3–12. The
teacher states a number either at random, or initially, in
sequence. If the pupil's card number is a factor of that
number, he/she stands up. If it is not a factor, he/she sits
down. If some pupils are not paying attention, shout 'Swap!'
and pupils must swap cards with each other before resuming.

100. Magic chairs

What you need: 5 chairs in a row
Subject links: speaking and listening, numeracy

✦ Create a row of five chairs. Three players sit side by side at
one end of the row. Their objective is to occupy all three
seats at the other end of the row in as few a number of
moves as possible. They may move either sideways one space
into an empty chair or leapfrog over another player into an
empty chair. They cannot leapfrog over two players in one
move. The least number of moves possible is four.

✦ A simple investigation could be recorded graphically by
changing the number of chairs and exploring the minimal
number of moves required.

101. **Fractions**

What you need: for Fraction Decimal Percentage Card Throw, cards displaying fractions, decimals, visual image, ratio, percentage equivalences. For Dominoes for Fractions, Decimals and Percentages, domino cards displaying fractions or decimals or percentages or ratios. For Fraction Recipe, real-life recipes that state numbers of people served.
Subject links: numeracy

✦ FRACTION DECIMAL PERCENTAGE CARD THROW
Once pupils understand the principle of equivalences, gather all the cards and throw them in the air. Pupils race in teams to match accurately all equivalences in the fastest possible time. A large number of cards will be required.

✦ DOMINOES FOR FRACTIONS, DECIMALS AND PERCENTAGES
If you do not possess a pack of these they would be easy to create on card and laminate, possibly by the class itself as they investigate equivalences. Play using standard rules for dominoes with the aim of placing all dominoes down on the table. Pick up a domino from the pile if you cannot go.

✦ FRACTION RECIPE
Using real-life recipes from websites or children's favourites from home, DT projects or historical/cultural and geographical links from a society studied, work out the fraction of a used recipe or the quantity of ingredients used by amending the proportions needed. How many people would be served by x quantity or how much of y ingredient is needed to serve z people?

102. Step estimation
What you need: measuring tape
Subject links: numeracy

✦ Pupils walk 10 steps and measure the total distance covered. Divide by 10 to find the average and convert from cm into m. Pupils then estimate the average for 20 steps and compare this with measuring an actual 20 step walk.

103. Team clocks
What you need: 1–12 number cards, short ropes, long ropes, optional PE cones
Subject links: numeracy, speaking and listening

✦ Divide the class into teams. Pupils hold number cards in an inward facing circle to create a clock face. One pupil stands in the centre holding the ends of both a longer and shorter rope. Two more pupils hold the other ends of the ropes, one as a minute hand and the other as the hour hand.

✦ A variations to this exercise would be simply to place number cards in a circle. Pairs of pupils arrange both ropes to show the time stated by the teacher.

✦ Ideally, complete this in a large space to allow a lot of physical movement as pupils compete to arrange analogue clock faces called out by the teacher.

104. **Axis co-ordinates Twister**®

What you need: large prepared grid with positive and negative x and y axis
Subject links: numeracy

✦ Play this game in the same way as standard Twister®, using a simple spinner with left/right, hand/foot combinations to be placed on co-ordinates, eg (2, -1) or (-3, -4), etc. Only have numbers 1–5 along axis to ensure numbers called out are not too far apart to cause injury. Call co-ordinates from the spinner or from specially labelled dice.

✦ As an extension, pairs could work at symmetry using an axis as their line of symmetry. One player must symmetrically match his/her team mate as he/she moves according to the spinner. To avoid entanglements, have one player use positive numbers only, and the other negative only.

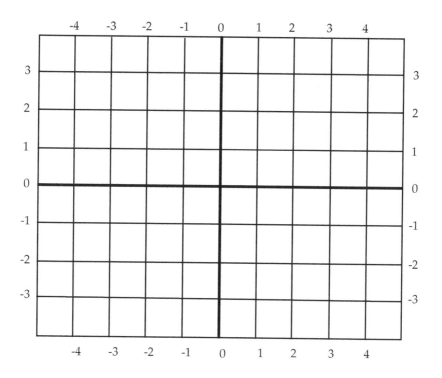

Science

105. Transparent, translucent and opaque

What you need: nothing
Subject links: science

✦ When explaining to pupils the differences between the three above terms, provide them with two minutes to find an example of a transparent material in the classroom.

✦ Repeat the process for the other material types. Include worn materials. Most classrooms contain plenty of examples of each material type. This enables movement and discovery in what can be a very dry topic.

✦ Pupils can then list the practical examples and uses of different materials, explaining why an item is designed utilizing that property.

106. **Life-sized paper skeleton**

What you need: paper, sticky tape
Subject links: science, DT

✦ In small teams make a life-sized paper skeleton of a member of the team. Measure the lengths of the member's body and use to cut out strips of paper the correct length. Label the body part on the 'bone' they represent. For the skull measure the jaw, circumference around the forehead, the top of skull, and from the bottom of the chin to the top of the head.

✦ Also measure the length of the back (from bottom of skull), chest, waist, shoulders to elbow and to wrist, hand span and length, hips to knees and to ankle, and the length of the feet.

✦ Compare bone lengths. As an extension, pupils could speculate and predict the longest and shortest lengths they might find. More advanced pupils could also find the true names of the major bones and label these onto their own skeleton.

107. **Earth, Moon and Sun**

What you need: cards indicating the Earth, Moon and Sun. Optional cards for other planets and time periods
Subject links: science, numeracy

✦   Divide the class into groups of three. Model the orbit of the Earth around the Sun, and that of the Moon around the Earth. Give pupils a name or picture card to indicate their role so they can then enact the orbits. Remember the Sun remains stationary, the Earth spins anticlockwise on its axis around the Sun, and the Moon orbits with the same side always facing the Earth.

✦   Extensions: include references to time. One Earth orbit around the Sun = 365.25 days. A lunar orbit of the Earth = 28 days. A complete spin of the Earth on its axis = 1 Earth day.

✦   Additionally you could add the other seven planets in their orbits around the Sun. In order from the Sun out they comprise Mercury, Venus, Earth, Mars, Jupiter, Saturn, Uranus and finally Neptune. (Note: Pluto is no longer classified as a true planet, being too small, and was the first in a new category called 'minor planets' of which there are a few in our solar system.)

108. Exploring nature

What you need: hula hoops, paper and pencils, plastic cups, mirrors, blindfolds, card, double-sided or looped sticky tape
Subject links: science

✦   QUADRANT
Identify and record the number and type of species within a meter square. Alternatively cast a hula hoop to mark the study area. Compare a variety of surfaces: paving slabs, grassed areas, under trees, edge of ponds, within bushes, etc.

✦   NATURE SYMPHONY
How many natural sounds can pupils hear? Which natural 'instruments' can they identify and name?

✦   SMELLY COCKTAILS
Children collect any plants found within the school grounds. Add the leaves and permitted flowers to a plastic cup. Add a little water and crush/mix together. Stir hard to release the smell. Stand the class in a circle and pass cups to the left until all have had a smell. Ensure cups are labelled first to enable the winner of the smelliest cocktail to be identified.

✦   MEET THE TREES
In pairs, pupils blindfold their partners and guide them to a tree. When they arrive, the guide warns the blindfolded child where the tree is so that he/she doesn't bump into it. The blindfolded partner hugs the tree. He/she may feel and touch around the roots, stretching as high as possible. He/she is then led back to the start and has to identify which tree it was by looking, inspecting and remembering the touch and layout of the branches, its texture, etc. (Double check for nettles and thorns first.)

- ✦ **NATURE PALLET**
  Provide each pupil with a card with double-sided sticky tape attached, and see how many colours pupils can gather from nature on this pallet. The activity is best completed during a short walk around the school to encounter different plant types.

- ✦ **EYE IN THE SKY**
  With mirrors held under the nose and the pupil's free arm on the shoulder of the pupil in front, lead the group through a flat path in a wooded area to get an alternative view of the canopy, sky and tops of buildings.

109. **Junior field studies**

What you need: large light coloured sheet, recording sheet, pooters (tool to suck up bugs into sealed container). Optional: watering can, and spade, pens, colours, paper
Subject links: science

✦   MINIBEASTS COMPARISON
Compare grassland, woodland and water wildlife. Use a 'tree shake' to gather beasts. Pupils hold out large white sheet to catch falling creatures whilst other pupils or adults vigorously shake a tree or bush.

✦   Kick sampling may also be used. Simply kick up large clods of earth and examine the creatures found within the soil. Alternatively, you could dig up a soil section with a spade. Create pupils' own keys to identify creatures discovered.

✦   WORM CHARMING
Use a watering can to rain on the soil area selected. Pupils tap the ground with any type of rhythm to draw worms to the surface.

History

110. Kinaesthetic history ideas

What you need: collage material, glue, pencils; for Photo Collage, photographs of pupils. For Costumes, card human outline. For Artefacts, real or replica artefacts
Subject links: history, DT, PE, art geography, RE, literacy

✦ PHOTO COLLAGE
Cut out the head from a photograph of the pupil, who then creates a collage costume or body for him/herself based upon the topic. Encourage the pupils to pick out and illustrate rich, accurate historical detail.

✦ COSTUMES
Pupils equip a card human outline with the necessary kit and clothing to fulfil their role, eg Scott of Antarctic, Willy Wonka, a Roman soldier. Pay lots of attention to accurate detail such as chain mail, weapons, tools, etc.

✦ SPORTS
Pupils conduct research with the teacher, demonstrate with the rest of the class, and try out historical sports of an era or society studied. This is a very useful way of engaging reluctant boys in research, history, RE or geography.

✦ RECIPES
Write instructions for and make a historically accurate food. Discuss why certain ingredients were used (historical/geographical context) and the healthiness of the food for us.

✦ ARTEFACTS
Pupils handle, feel and investigate artefacts without being told what they are. They could jot down in note form any ideas, questions or suggestions they have about what the object is, how it is used and who uses it. What does it tell us about people's lives? This could be used as a start point for descriptive writing.

111. **What really happened?**

What you need: exciting text or video footage
Subject links: history, RE, literacy, geography, PSHE

✦ Act out an event from history, geography, RE, etc INCORRECTLY. Pupils must identify the error and state or demonstrate the correct version.

Geography

112. **Inflatable globes**

What you need: inflatable globe, check sheet (see below)
Subject links: geography

✦ Call out a letter of the alphabet and throw a beach ball style inflatable globe to a pupil. When the child catches the globe they must say a country beginning with that letter. The next child to be thrown the globe must find a country beginning with the next letter, and so on. All letters other than X have a country beginning with that letter. In order that pupils expand upon their awareness of the difference between countries and continents, they should also state which continent the country is on, or which ocean surrounds it for island states.

✦ For many letters there is a wide range of countries from which to choose. The chart below gives a sample country for each letter (except X). Encourage children to find other countries starting with the appropriate letter.

A	B	C	D	E
Australia	Brazil	Canada	Denmark	Egypt
Oceania	South America	North America	Europe	Africa
F	**G**	**H**	**I**	**J**
France	Germany	Honduras	India	Japan
Europe	Europe	North America	Asia	Asia
K	**L**	**M**	**N**	**O**
Kenya	Libya	Madagascar	New Zealand	Oman
Africa	Africa	Africa	Oceania	Asia
P	**Q**	**R**	**S**	**T**
Poland	Qatar	Russia	Spain	Thailand
Europe	Asia	Europe/Asia	Europe	Asia
U	**V**	**W**	**Y**	**Z**
United Kingdom	Venezuela	Western Samoa	Yemen	Zambia
Europe	South America	Oceania	Asia	Africa

113. **Geography Twister®**
What you need: map and spinner
Subject links: geography

✦   Create a large floor map of either the world or Europe. Label the main countries or the continents. You may wish to include the main seas and oceans too. Create a basic spinner labelled with left hand, right hand, left foot and right foot. Call out the name of the location to be touched and the body part to be used. The objective is to make your opponent fall over in as few a number of moves possible. The winner is the one to stay balanced on their limbs as long as possible.

114. **Compass bearings**
What you need: nothing
Subject links: geography, mathematics

✦   This task helps pupils link the points of the compass in relation to one another. Label children as compass bearings (north, south, east and west). The teacher determines which wall in the classroom is north. The pupils then arrange themselves to point in the correct direction for their bearing.

✦   This could be made more complex by using larger groups of eight children, including the labels north west, north east, south west and south east.

115. International signposts

What you need: compass, atlases
Subject links: geography, numeracy

✦ Make pupils aware of the points on a compass in relation to their classroom. Pupils then make a signpost with labels stuck on to indicate the correct distance from the classroom to school, local, national and international locations. Use maps to gauge direction and distance from the school of local features, holiday resorts, UK cities, other countries, etc.

MFL

116. Kinaesthetic MFL ideas

What you need: physical resources applicable to vocabulary used, eg clothes, actual food to touch, smell and taste
Subject links: MFL

✦ CLOTHES
Pupils will retain more vocabulary by using as many senses as possible to encounter new words. If learning about clothes, pupils could physically put on items of clothing they describe in conversation and feel the texture on their body. Pupils then write down the correctly spelt word in the MFL on the board or in their books to help reinforce written vocabulary.

✦ FOOD
Where practical, repeat the process used for clothes with food. Investigate the smells, textures and tastes of sample foods. Pupils should say the words out loud then write them down.

✦ SPORTS/PHYSICAL ACTIVITIES
Use mime to reinforce terminology.

117. MFL Twister®

What you need: for Finger Twister, A4 laminated worksheet displaying coloured shapes. For Body Parts Twister®, a Twister® game.
Subject links: MFL

✦   FINGER TWISTER
For finger twister use a laminated A4 worksheet displaying coloured shapes. The teacher calls the name of a colour and a shape, eg 'blue square', in the appropriate language. Pupils sit around a desk together and race to place their finger on the appropriate coloured shape on the worksheet. This hand remains in place as a second shape is called out. If pupils have small hand spans allow them to use both hands. Variations could be created using number squares or 100 squares.

✦   BODY PARTS TWISTER
For this activity use a traditional Twister® game. Reinforce colour, shape and body parts terminology by playing in the appropriate MFL. The teacher calls out any body part of his/her choosing, not just that on the spinner. School-made twister boards could include many new colours and shapes, such as orange, purple, gold, stars, crosses, etc.

RE

118. Physical prayer

What you need: space for dancing to take place (RE lesson/prayer time in hall?)
Subject links: PE, RE

✦   Use mime or dance as a means of spiritual expression. Use as part of prayer time in faith schools. Thinking time is needed to plan/identify what and how pupils could pray. Ideally this can be incorporated into dance units of PE, particularly in faith schools.

PE

119. **Instant PE lesson**

What you need: nothing at a pinch. Better with: cones, 4 footballs, 4 basket/net balls, mats, 4 tennis rackets and balls. For Assault Course, hula hoops, benches, mats. Simply use what is quickly and easily available
Subject links: PE

✦ WARM UP TRAFFIC LIGHTS
When the teacher shouts out a colour, pupils must respond instantly with the correct activity:

Red =	Stop
Orange =	Jog on spot
Green =	Go/run or hop, crawl, etc

✦ RELAY RACES
Four teams (use houses to avoid arguments) line up at one end of the hall/yard. They race through cones, either weaving in between, or through slalom style gates from one end of the hall/yard to the other and back to their team mates to release the next player to go. Teams could also dribble a football, bounce a basketball, hop to the end on one leg and return hopping on the other, balance a ball on a racket, shuttle run, etc.

✦ ASSAULT COURSE
If time and apparatus are available, set up a simple assault course: hula hoops (must pass through a hoop to continue the journey), climbing over, under or through benches or horses, crawling or doing sausage rolls across a mat. Provided it is safe, let your imagination run a little wild. Ask the class to suggest their own preferred variations, and either model these to the class or set up the equipment needed.

120. PE science

What you need: mats, benches, + and – stickers
Subject links: science, PE

✦ Use as a warm-up to a PE lesson as a means of reinforcing what has been studied in science.

✦ PULLING AND PUSHING FORCES
Pupils use mats and benches to travel, only utilizing pushes and pulls to move. Pupils could be encouraged to create the most original push and pull motions.

✦ MAGNETS
Divide pupils into positive and negative poles. Use + and – stickers to indicate polarity. Similar charges would repel each other and opposites would attract. Emphasize the need to remain 'pushed' away from like poles and 'pulled' towards opposites. Stress the need to be responsible for your own movement and NOT to push or pull other pupils.

PSHE

121. Friendly words

What you need: paper, sticky tape, pens
Subject links: PSHE, RE

✦ Tape a sheet of paper to the back of each child. The pupils move around the classroom and write one word describing a positive attribute on that pupil's paper sheet on their back.

✦ To encourage a equal number of comments, provide a limit of either the class size (one comment from each pupil), or a lower limit with a rule that the same word cannot be repeated twice. The latter will encourage pupils to think more broadly about a pupil's contribution and characteristics, and to expand their vocabulary.

General

122. Team raps and poems

What you need: nothing (option to write/display for class participation)
Subject links: any

✦   TEAM RAP
As a whole class, or as a paired or individual exercise, produce a rap to assist retaining information relevant to a topic. Emphasize extra marks for effective use of any keywords or formulas. Raps can also be used in class or school assemblies to reinforce learning in a 'cool' way.

✦   TEAM POEM
Similar to a rap, write a poem or limerick about the studied topic, focusing upon keywords or formulas to reinforce learning. It may be helpful to provide a word bank as a prompt.

123. Topic singing

What you need: CD and player
Subject links: any, music

✦   Write new lyrics to a song that is popular and easy to sing by the entire class. Ideally, use a song that you have the music for on CD as a backing track. Teams write their own words to the song to revise topic knowledge. Display the lyrics, sing them all together and vote for the version that best uses words relating to the topic.

124. Mistakes

What you need: passage with prepared 'errors'
Subject links: any

✦ Slowly read out a passage which contains deliberate mistakes. As they listen, pupils should note the errors and write down the correct facts instead. Pupils could then indicate the correct answers either by voting with a show of hands for the correct answer, or by using their personal whiteboards to all display the correct answers together.

✦ The incorrect passage may also be written on a whiteboard or differentiated sheets. Pupils should investigate and discuss in teams what is incorrect and work together to use resources to make the necessary corrections. A time limit can be set.

125. Word and time boundary

What you need: nothing
Subject links: any

✦ Write a text about a given topic in EXACTLY 200 words or in EXACTLY 10 minutes.

✦ Alternatively, write down a clear definition in exactly 20 words. All words produced MUST make sense and be grammatically accurate.

126. Speaking challenges

What you need: nothing
Subject links: any

✦   CHAIN CHAT
Each pupil has 30 seconds to talk about the topic being studied, without repeating anything that was just said by the previous speakers. Ensure this is a whole class activity, and allow weaker pupils to speak earlier, once they have had time to engage their knowledge by having heard a couple of other speakers first.

✦   DESCRIBE THE ARTEFACT
Show one pupil an artefact hidden from the view of the rest of the class. The pupil then describes aloud what the item looks, smells and feels like without saying what the object is or what it is used for (too easy). The winner is the pupil able to describe the artefact well enough to enable pupils to identify it in the least number of guesses.

✦   FAST FACTS
Have the first ten pupils tell one fast fact each about the topic being studied. Make this exercise into a regular habit for the class as part of a plenary or as an introductory link at the start of the lesson. Encourage the pupils to listen carefully to each fast fact to:
- ❑   Ensure accurate facts are given
- ❑   Reinforce their own listening
- ❑   Reward each accurate or original fact
- ❑   Not repeat any answers given.

✦ QUESTION CHAIN
  Give pupils thinking time to develop some topic related
  knowledge. All pupils then stand, competing to be the last
  man standing. Select a pupil to ask a question and either the
  teacher or the original pupil asks another child to answer it.
  Limit the number of seconds response time allowed. Pupils
  sit down or lose a life if they run out of time or answer
  incorrectly.

127. **Hot seat mind map**

What you need: large sheets of paper, colour pens
Subject links: any

✦ Individuals or pairs sit in chairs at the front of the class and
  talk about a topic or a character in detail for 30 seconds.
  They may then be asked questions.

✦ The class mind maps on large sheets of paper in one colour
  what was revealed about the topic or character.

✦ The next pupil takes the hot seat and repeats the process,
  and the result is recorded on the mind maps, but this time in
  a different colour. Continue until the mind map is complete
  or until all pupils have had the chance to speak.

✦ Giving pupils individual areas to investigate will ensure
  that there are no topic or character areas left uncovered or
  unrecorded on the mind map.

128. Listening, writing and speaking games

What you need: paper, pens
Subject links: any

✦ BINGO
Best played on the pupils' own whiteboards, there are many possible variations of this popular game. Questions and answers can be related to any topic, eg chemical formulas, countries, times tables, grammatical terms, foreign words.

✦ CREATE A QUIZ
Pupils work in pairs to write down five original and interesting questions to which they know the answers. They then select their top two questions and write them down on a piece of paper with the answers on the reverse. Questions from all pairs are then drawn out of a hat. Read out the best questions only as a quiz whilst pupils write down their answers. By having two questions per paper you can read out the best from each and avoid duplicate questions.

✦ TRUMP CARDS
Pupils create a deck of cards from the same topic linked by a theme, eg WW2 aircraft, statistics about countries or mountain ranges, ruling monarchs. Ensure each deck of cards contains statistics relating to a few or more agreed categories, eg body weight, air speed, age span, longest river, etc. Pupils then play in pairs or larger groups.

✦　　There are a variety of ways this game can be played. The most common is for all cards to be distributed equally between players. The first player calls a category for their chosen card (one in which that card is highly ranked). The other players must then put down the top card from their hand. The player with the highest statistic in the category called then wins all the played cards and places them at the back of his/her deck.

✦　　The winner takes his/her top card and determines which category to call. Repeat the process for a set time limit or until only one player has cards left. This is an ideal game for taking outside or for use during wet play.

129. Name hat

What you need: each pupil's name written on identically sized cards, colour coded for house
Subject links: any

✦　　Create a quiz bank of questions.

✦　　Increase the amount of competition in the class and encourage house competitions. Too often questions are answered by the same pupils. Avoid this by drawing name cards out of a hat or tin at random. The pupil picked must then answer the question. Colour coding the name cards by house will increase house competition and increase support for fellow house members.

✦　　Reward two points for each correct answer, but allow a one point rescue by any member of the house who is able to answer correctly instead. If neither answer correctly, open the question to the other houses to answer for one point.

Literacy

130. **Word pairs**

What you need: nothing
Subject links: literacy, geography, history, MFL

✦ Divide the class into pairs. Either at the front of the class or working across the classroom, the first pupil says a verb. The second pupil must then say an adverb to accompany the first, eg swimming + rapidly. These words could be thematic and prepared in advance by the teacher. The categories may also refer to nouns (objects or characters). In this case, the second pupil must state an adjective to accompany the initial noun, eg volcano + erupting.

✦ An additional variation could see one 'Word Master' choose the initial word with three pupils competing against him/her. The three competitors must come up with their own responses without repeating their teammates' words. Pupils could refer to artefacts, locations, characters and their characteristics, etc, including the use of MFL. (Once colours and numbers are secure it may be best to ban their use from the game.)

✦ Allow only five seconds for the second pupil to answer. Disallow any exclamation or 'umming' prior to answering, any repetition, and any incorrect words that do not match the criteria or word type.

131. **Book team**

What you need: printed outline of a sports pitch
Subject links: literacy

✦ Pupils race to complete an entire sports team of players to encourage reading diversity of different genres and formats. Each position for their squad is filled when pupils complete a book from a specific genre, eg biographies = striker, science fiction = defender. Pupils are allowed to choose their own sport or other 'targets' for their genre rewards.

✦ Some sports may not have the exact number of positions compared to the genre range available. This could be amended by pupils determining which style of writing they may find the most difficult, and agreeing to a reward of gaining two players when completed. For pupils who favour individual sports, positions, strikes or serves may be used instead, eg back-hand, left hook, 50m hurdle, etc.

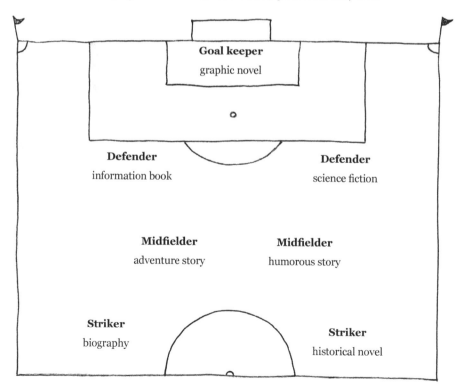

Goal keeper

graphic novel

Defender

information book

Defender

science fiction

Midfielder

adventure story

Midfielder

humorous story

Striker

biography

Striker

historical novel

132. Land's End to John O'Groats reading race

What you need: map of Great Britain with small towns visible
Subject links: literacy

✦ Encourage a purpose and competition to reading through setting up this race for pupils to win. Each page a pupil reads in a standard text could gain 1km or more as determined by the teacher. These towns listed below are theoretically 50km apart and should be treated as stages rather than true distances. Small prizes, such as stickers, house points or golden time could be awarded as acknowledgements and encouragement.

✦ 1407 km is the actual road distance between John O'Groats and Land's End. The route as the crow flies passes over the sea on a few occasions. This list of 30 towns and cities on the most direct road route would result in a new stage being passed approximately every 50km. You can find these on most UK maps:

❏ John O'Groats
❏ Wick
❏ Helmsdale
❏ Tain
❏ Inverness
❏ Aviemore
❏ Pitlochry
❏ Perth
❏ Stirling
❏ Glasgow
❏ Moffat
❏ Carlisle
❏ Penrith
❏ Lancaster
❏ Preston
❏ Manchester
❏ Stoke-on-Trent

- ☐ Cannock
- ☐ Birmingham
- ☐ Worcester
- ☐ Gloucester
- ☐ Bristol
- ☐ Taunton
- ☐ Exeter
- ☐ Plymouth
- ☐ Truro
- ☐ Penzance
- ☐ Land's End

✦ This could be adapted to become a race across the Solar System, Europe or the World, as the distances for stages and rewards can easily be changed.

✦ Ideally a map with moveable name stickers could be displayed showing and encouraging progress. This also allows teachers to follow pupils' reading progress at a glance.

133. **Races**

What you need: pupil copies of text, dictionaries
Subject links: literacy

✦   SKIMMING RACE
The teacher chooses a word from a class text and writes it and the page number on the board. Pupils race to find the word. The first pupil with his/her hand up should be chosen to read the sentence aloud to confirm the find. Repeat. In groups pupils could take turns to find a word and inform the group of the word and page number. Rotate around the table.

✦   DICTIONARY RACE
Play either as the entire class or as individual ability groups or tables. The teacher states a word, clearly enunciated from the dictionary. Pupils then find the word in the dictionary using their phonic and spelling skills. The first pupil per class or group reads aloud the definition correctly to win.

134. **Secret definition**

What you need: several slips of paper per pupil, pencils
Subject links: literacy

✦   The teacher says a word aloud and writes it down on the board. Pupils, either individually or in pairs, must then write down on a slip of paper what they believe is the meaning of the word.

✦   Encourage the investigation of prefixes and syllables to break down the word into a definition. Read aloud the responses. Reward the most accurate, and possibly the funniest, definitions for each word.

135. Envoy

What you need: nothing
Subject links: any, speaking and listening

✦ Divide the class into groups, ideally with the same number of children as there are groups, eg a class of 25 pupils would have five groups of five pupils. Each group then works together to investigate its own topic. When all research is completed an envoy is sent, one at a time, to a different group to find out about its research. The envoy then feedbacks to his/her original group.

✦ A different envoy is then selected and sent to a different team to discover what they have investigated and then the pupil reports back to the original team. This continues until all team members have visited and reported back from a different group so that each original team has full feedback on all investigations.

✦ You could add time limits, to make the activity more competitive.

Numeracy

136. **Football pitch multiplication**

What you need: laminated printouts of a football pitch (may be printed off some interactive whiteboards), colour cubes in chosen team colours
Subject links: numeracy

✦ Divide pupils into pairs. They should take their printout of the football pitch and draw a grid on it that contains enough squares for them to write in each one the times tables they know, but without the answers, eg 4 x 8. The pupils then choose their different team colours and take those colour cubes. Flip a coin to determine who starts the game.

✦ The start player, with possession of an imaginary ball, places his/her cube in the centre and aims to move towards the opposition goal by correctly answering the times table question written on each square. The player's own colour cube is placed on every square for a correct answer. A goal is scored and recorded if the cubes make a continuous link from the middle of the pitch to the opposition goal. If an error is made, possession of the imaginary ball passes to the opposing team who starts in turn from the centre and repeats the process.

✦ If no further moves are possible by either team, remove all the cubes from the pitch and count it as a victory for the team with the most goals scored, resume with new questions drawn onto the squares, or simply switch the pitch around as in half time.

✦ The pitches could be reused if they are laminated after the squares have been drawn on them. Pupils can write the sums using whiteboard pens and wipe them off to play again.

137. **Physical pairs**
What you need: pairs cards
Subject links: numeracy

✦ Play the matching pairs game as a team challenge. Place pairs cards face down on the floor. Pupils sit in a circle around them. The criteria of the pairs could be timestables, time, fractions, number bonds, equivalent weights and measures, etc. Pupils turn over the cards, two at a time, to find pairs. When a matching pair is found the matching cards are removed from the floor. The team with the most matches wins.

✦ This can be differentiated simply by leaving the cards face upwards, making a match easier.

138. **Number line: connect 3**
What you need: 10 sided dice, number line, colour pens or markers
Subject links: numeracy

✦ Support reading number lines and/or estimation using this exercise. Divide the class into pairs. Players choose a coloured pen each and take turns to roll two or more dice. They use the digits from the dice to create a decimal. The player then marks that place correctly on the number line in their colour. Incorrect marking is disallowed and removed from the number line. The second player then repeats the process for his/her turn. The winner is the first person with three numbers marked consecutively on the line in his/her colour.

✦ Variations can be created: use three dice not two for two decimal places, or increase the consecutive numbers needed in line to four or more.

MFL

139. MFL ideas

✦ SIMON SAYS
A great, quick game for reinforcing action words and/or body parts.

✦ EYE SPY
Reinforce classroom vocabulary using this traditional game. This might be useful on coach trips, visits or even in the school playground if there is a good view of local features.

✦ MFL FIZZ BUZZ
All pupils stand and the objective is to be the last man standing. Pupils call out one number progressing sequentially around the room, eg '1', '2', '3' etc. When a number ends in a certain digit, eg '5', pupils say 'fizz' instead of the number. When the number ends in a different digit, eg '0', pupils say 'buzz' instead. So counting would go: '4', 'fizz', '6', '7', '8', '9', 'buzz', '11', etc.

✦ This continues through the higher numbers and includes those ending in 5 or 0. Play through initially in English if pupils are unfamiliar with the game, and then in the MFL.

✦ MFL WARM UP
Ensure numbers or other vocabulary from recent MFL teaching are displayed around the sides of the hall or playground. When the teacher calls out the number or word, pupils race to be the first to touch the side it is displayed upon. Have multiple numbers or images for each side or use marked areas or coloured lines on the ground instead.

140. **MFL noughts and crosses**
What you need: 3 x 3 grid, images of topic vocabulary
Subject links: MFL

✦ Sketch a 3 x 3 grid on the board that contains nine images of topic-based vocabulary.

✦ Two teams compete to win at noughts and crosses by naming the object or answering a question about the topic in the spaces of the 3 x 3 grid. Teams can choose which space to complete first.

141. **Numbers, colours, shapes and letters**
What you need: large (A3+) laminated sheets, marked with colour shapes (yellow triangles, red circles, etc)
Subject links: MFL

✦ Display the sheet marked with colour shapes. The teacher calls out a colour shape. Pupils then compete to slap the correct one. This is best played with four pupils or so around a desk. It is a simple game practising fast reactions while reinforcing colours or shapes. It can be extended and mixed to focus upon the spoken alphabet, numbers and other topic vocabulary.

142. Colour 'fruit'

What you need: fruit flavoured pastels of assorted colours (wrappers on!)
Subject links: MFL

✦ Hide a coloured sweet in your hand. Pupils have to enquire in the appropriate language what the fruit is, eg 'Is the fruit red?', 'Is the fruit an apple?' By listening to other pupils and using deduction pupils can win the 'fruit'. Ensure universal participation by rotating between pupils, with one question only per pupil.

143. MFL faces

What you need: For Guess Who®, board game. For Happy Families, cards (either purchased or school made)
Subject links: MFL

✦ GUESS WHO?®
Guess Who?® is an existing board game where pupils have to deduce the identity of a chosen individual from a hidden array of faces. This game requires knowledge of, or quick access to, vocabulary of skin, eye and hair colour, clothing worn on the head or torso, glasses and jewellery.

✦ HAPPY FAMILIES
Happy families is a card game with sets of four cards per family which pupils attempt to collect. Pupils could create a family each. Traditionally this game has a Mum, Dad, Son and Daughter in each pack referred to as Mr X, Mrs X, Master X and Miss X. The family surname is usually linked to a profession.

144. **Last man standing**

What you need: nothing
Subject links: MFL

✦   A game for whole class participation. The objective is to be
the last man standing. Pupils count up starting from zero
in the MFL. They may call out up to three numbers. Any
number ending in zero spoken by a pupil means he/she has
to sit down and be out. Pupils may say one, two or three
numbers in sequence, eg '6' or '6, 7' or '6, 7, 8'. The next pupil
has to continue the sequence. Pupils may decide to say one,
two or three numbers depending upon who they wish to get
out or keep in the game.

✦   For younger pupils you may have to provide a ceiling on
the size of numbers used. Return to zero at the end of
the sequence. Continue playing until only one pupil is left
standing. It may be useful to play the game in English first so
pupils grasp the rules prior to playing in a MFL.

Geography

145. Map symbol snap

What you need: key to map symbols, card, colour pencils, pens
Subject links: geography

✦ Pupils produce their own matching pairs cards by accurately drawing the symbols from map keys and, on a different card, writing in words the meaning for that symbol. Pupils then turn all cards face down and play to find matching pairs within a time limit. The one with the most matching pairs wins.

146. Treasure hunt

What you need: laminated maps of the school grounds, dry marker pens, suitable colour coded treasures for different teams
Subject links: geography, PE

✦ Divide pupils into teams; each team will need a laminated map of the school grounds. The teams hide the weatherproof treasures (possibly laminated tags or colour specific small pieces of PE equipment) and use dry marker pens to record the locations on their maps. When complete they exchange maps with other teams and race to discover other teams' hidden treasures within a time limit.

PE

147. **Magic stick**

What you need: metre sticks or similar, stopwatch (optional)
Subject links: PE, PSHE

✦ This team game is very funny if the rules are followed. Two or more teams must form two lines with team members facing each other with hands at waist height, forefinger extended on both hands to support the stick. CONTACT WITH THE STICK MUST BE MAINTAINED AT ALL TIMES BY EVERYONE'S FINGERS. The aim is to lower the stick to the floor in the shortest amount of time. You must ensure that each team maintains finger contact in order for this to be a fair competition.

✦ To keep a close eye on the team, have one team play at a time, and use a stopwatch to time the teams.

✦ The emphasis is on communication since there is a tendency to allow the stick to rise rather than lower. This can result in either laughter or arguments, or both, depending on the teams.

148. **Roll out**

What you need: rope, large light ball, lots of beanbags
Subject links: PE

✦   Divide the class into four teams. Place a large, light ball in the centre of a square and have the teams surround it, one on each side of the square. Equip each team with an equal number of bean bags. The teams' objective is to hit the ball with the bags so that it rolls towards and touches an opposing team's side. A point is scored against the team whose side is touched by the ball. The team with the LEAST points wins.

✦   Variations:
- All pupils throw the bags at will
- One team at a time throws the bags
- One pupil at a time throws the bags.

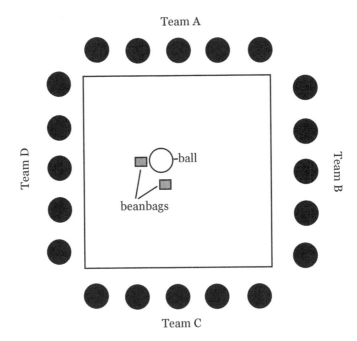

PSHE

149. **Head down, thumbs up**

What you need: nothing
Subject links: PSHE

✦　　Pupils all sit in their places. Four pupils are selected to be 'on'. All other pupils place their heads down on their desks with their eyes closed and their thumbs up, resting their hands on the desk. The four chosen pupils move quietly around the room and each gently pinch any one pupil on the thumb. They then return to the front of the classroom and call out 'Stand if pinched.' The four seated pupils who were pinched on the thumb then stand. Teacher then calls out their names one at a time for them to say who they thought pinched their thumb. If they guess correctly they swap seats with the pupil who was previously 'on'. When all four pupils have guessed, continue with a new game.

✦　　A variation could include all the pinched pupils having to stand behind the person they believe has pinched them. After all four pupils are standing in place, the correct guessers remain in place and the others sit down.

General

150. Setting goals and providing feedback

What you need: nothing
Subject links: any

✦   DRAFTING SUCCESS CRITERIA
Encourage pupils to develop and draft success criteria as part of a whole class discussion. Ownership of these criteria could build confidence and increase pupils' checking progress of their own work and development against the criteria. Peer evaluation could also use the success criteria.

✦   THREE STARS AND A WISH
Pupils exchange or observe other pupils' work. They then analyse how the other pupil is performing. Feedback is then modelled or given directly to the class or to the producer of the work. The format is three positive points (the stars) and one area (the wish) to develop for next time.

✦   It may be useful for work that is of high quality to be scanned and displayed on the whiteboard or photocopied. Pupils can underline in colour or highlight their own three stars and circle or write down their wish.

151. **Speaking games**

What you need: topic knowledge, lists of forbidden words
Subject links: any

✦   POSITIVE, MINUS, INTERESTING (PMI)
    Initiate high order group or individual discussion by
    proposing a conundrum to the class, eg if school pencils were
    made from chocolate what would be the consequences?
    Each pair or team would be awarded points by the teacher,
    class and themselves for the issues they raised for each
    positive, minus and interesting item. Conundrums could
    be based upon topics being studied or could be purely
    imaginative to stimulate skills of logic and high order
    thinking.

✦   TABOO
    Describe a person, artefact or technique without saying the
    actual name. Use role-play and hand gestures to indicate
    what you are describing in addition to verbal descriptions.
    To make this more challenging, ban certain give-away words
    from being used to force both listeners and players to really
    think about the topic. Timers could also be used to find
    winners and the best teams.

152. **Group discussion**

What you need: pencils and paper per group
Subject links: speaking and listening, science, RE, PSHE, history

✦ Working in groups of five is less intimidating than a large group or whole class discussion and may allow less confident children to express themselves. By allocating roles to each of the five children, they can be kept on task even in friendship groups. The roles:

❒ CHAIR: keeps discussion on task. Organizes the group if required.

❒ SCRIBE: notes down key points and checks they have written the group's responses.

❒ REPORTER: Works with the scribe to sum up and share group ideas with the class.

❒ ENCOURAGER: Helps group members express themselves, encouraging participation from quiet ones.

❒ OBSERVER: Notes how well the group worked, sharing this at the end for the group to discuss how well they worked together and how they may improve next time.

153. **Questions**
What you need: nothing
Subject links: any

✦   CLASS QUESTIONS
The class discuss what they have learnt so far within a topic. Pairs or groups then write down as many questions as possible related to the topic. The teacher then selects the best questions for possible class investigation or testing.

✦   WHAT'S THE QUESTION?
Provide the answers to a topic being studied and have pupils deduce what the question is, eg 'Moscow': What is the capital of Russia; 'Scorpion King': Who was the first ruler of Egypt? Try to avoid answers for which there are multiple possible questions. This activity is best completed as part of an assessment towards the end of a unit.

154. **Board game**
What you need: topic knowledge
Subject links: any

✦   Pupils create their own board game based upon what they have learnt in a topic, eg the Spanish Armada, escape from villains in a studied text, survival within an ecosystem, travel around the body, etc.

✦   Ensure that the pupils use correct terminology, spellings and real topic detail to engage with the topic in some depth.

155. **Storytelling and debating**

What you need: optional musical instruments, tape/MP3 recorder
Subject links: literacy, RE, history, geography, music, ICT

✦ DEBATES
Dividing the class into opposite camps and holding debates
can enliven many topics, eg should Julius Caesar invade or
not? You could also use this technique to encourage and
springboard scientific investigations and understanding: This
class believes that ALL metals are magnetic. True or false?

✦ PERSONIFIED TALE
Provide pupils with an outline of an adventure story where
they are the main character, as a human, water droplet, fish/
animal, machine, etc. Going around the class pupils use their
topic knowledge and imagination to state in 30 seconds what
happens next to the character. The focus is upon aural story
telling including lots of accurate facts about what would
happen to the character, eg kidnapped by Vikings, falling
from a cloud as a raindrop, swimming upstream to spawn,
etc.

✦ RADIO PLAY
A calmer version of role-play is to use voice only to
dramatize an event or discovery. It is important for pupils
to plan not just what to say but also HOW to say it, using
punctuation for emphasis. Include sound effects and
recordings if possible. Almost any topic could be covered, eg
the arrival of the Romans in Britain, dramatized literature,
Biblical event, travelogues, etc.

✦ SOUND AND SONG STORY
Retell the tale without words. Use sound only to recount
the main events in the story. Pupils could write their own
lyrics, perhaps to the existing music from a well-known song,
recounting the tale.

156. **Soundtrack**

What you need: web video or DVD, audio book on CD
Subject links: literacy

✦ Play a video or DVD, but without the visual image (switch to No Show or close down the projector). Listen to the soundtrack only. Pupils should concentrate upon hearing clues to develop ideas about characters, settings, imagery, etc.

157. **Gathering information**

What you need: for Jigsaw Listening, text read by teacher. For Survey, clipboards, pupil-prepared surveys, pens
Subject links: speaking and listening, literacy geography, PSHE

✦ JIGSAW LISTENING
The teacher reads a passage a number of times over at a steady pace. At the first reading all children merely listen. In later readings, however, they may make notes, focusing upon key words and phrases. Their task will be to reiterate the information from the spoken text. It does not have to be exact quotes. After the readings pupils pair up, compare notes by discussion and expand what they now share. Two pairs now join into a group of four, aiming to include all the information from the original text in written form.

✦ SURVEY
In pairs or groups, pupils compile a survey upon the topic studied to ask either in class, in the playground during lunch, or at home. This exercise is especially good for local issues such as citizenship or geography, eg proposed local development, compulsory healthy eating in schools, etc.

158. **Fact, opinion or belief?**

What you need: nothing
Subject links: literacy, science, RE, speaking and listening, PSHE, history, art, DT

✦ Identify facts, opinions and beliefs from areas of study.
These could include historical events, science observations,
health choices, examination of a design, religious duties, etc.
Create a dual list separating any raised issues into either fact
or opinion, determined by class discussion.

159. **Ask the author**

What you need: nothing
Subject links: literacy

✦ Pupils formulate questions to ask the author of a text
studied. Supported by the teacher, the class should attempt
to imagine themselves as the author and answer the
questions. An adult could hot seat the role as the author to
model the process of deduction. Alternatively, many authors'
websites now contain a questions and answers section, or
could perhaps be contacted by e-mail.

✦ As an extension, pupils could write a polite letter to the
author detailing what they have or have not enjoyed about
the story. They could suggest their own ideas for sequels or
additional plot devices.

160. **Text discussion**
What you need: class text
Subject links: literacy

✦ PROBLEM SOLVING
Read out a chapter from a story where a character faces a problem or danger. At a point in the text, stop reading. Separate the class into groups to discuss and record alternative solutions, including the likely consequences of each action.

✦ MINOR CHARACTER PERSPECTIVE
Retell a scene from a text in the first person from the view of a minor character.

✦ VILLAIN'S ROLE
Questions for class discussion: why are the villains acting as they are? What are their reasons or motives behind their actions?

✦ COMPARE AND CONTRAST
Evaluate any differences between the illustrations and the text. Upon a pupil's own reading of the text, do they imagine the scene or character any differently?

161. Personal responses

What you need: class texts
Subject links: literacy

✦ AUTHOR OR TOPIC
Discuss differences or similarities between books either
written by the same author, or on the same topic, read by
the pupil or the class.

✦ FAVOURITE SECTION
Pupils choose their happiest, most revealing, best illustrated,
most useful sections from the text and justify their choices.

✦ PERSONAL ACTION
Children say what they would have done themselves at a
stage in the story and explain their choices.

162. Wrong reading

What you need: set of books for class
Subject links: literacy

✦ Deliberately start reading a text without referencing the
cover, title, author or blurb. Read a chapter near the middle
of the book. Pupils have to discuss and decode what they
think is going on, who the main characters are and any ideas
about key features of the plot. Use as a means of introducing
a new text to the class. Record these ideas as a 'thought
shower' and review when the same chapter is later reached
following conventional reading.

163. **Prediction**
What you need: class text
Subject links: literacy

✦ Engage pupils with the text by providing a competitive purpose for reading. Explain the purpose of the competition. The class read a section of the text together. Pupils should provide an explanation as to what is happening and predict what will happen next. They should provide evidence for why they believe their predictions. At the end of the book, it would be interesting for pupils to review all their predictions and to see how close they were to what actually happened in the book. They should discuss what they have learnt from the exercise about prediction.

✦ For a group activity, while reading a shared text or class story, stop at an exciting moment. Pupils should close their books (if they have a copy) and in pairs or groups predict what they think may happen next, justifying their ideas from the text so far. Pupils could mime, imitate or act out a quick impression of what they believe will happen next.

164. **Alternative scene**
What you need: optional props
Subject links: literacy

✦ What would happen if... ? Freeze during a reading of a scenario and ask the pupils to consider what comes next OR to suggest alternatives. What would happen if X event was resolved differently, etc. Pupils then either act out the possible next scene OR simply suggest an alternative scenario instead. Pupils should base their predictions on evidence from the story.

165. **Alternative versions**

What you need: knowledge of a well-known or studied tale that can be adapted
Subject links: literacy

✦   CHANGES
    Change one key character in the story or one important decision taken by a character and rewrite the original tale with changed events and consequences.

✦   SWAP ROLES
    Make villains become heroes and vice versa.

✦   GENRE CHANGE
    Rewrite the same tale in the new format, eg put a historical tale into a contemporary setting.

✦   CHARACTER ADDITION AND SUBTRACTION
    Add or remove a character to affect the outcome of events.

✦   TITLES
    Determine names for numbered chapters or more exciting alternatives than those already used. They could also suggest alternative titles for books to make them sound more interesting, original or to practice alliteration.

✦   ENDINGS
    Write new chapter endings for the book. Keep all the details the same until that point. Establish some boundaries, such as only existing characters and plot devices should be used.

166. **Get to know your character**
What you need: character knowledge
Subject links: literacy, history

✦ CHARACTER DIARY
Break writing into smaller bite-sized chunks by encouraging
writing in the first-person voice of a character as a diary
entry. Write from the perspective of a piece of magma
moving toward the point of, and during the eruption from
a volcano; from the perspective of a Jedi knight or Spartan
soldier during their training; from the perspective of a plant,
animal and blood cell travelling around the body. Give extra
marks for including as much background information as
possible.

✦ Otherwise, write a detailed diary entry for one day from a
character's life. It may be best to use a key event from the
text or the day immediately before or after as the main
reference.

✦ CHARACTER KIT
Pupils produce a list of possessions that a character may have
owned, currently possesses or may desire to own or use in
the future. They must have evidence from the text justifying
their choices, including location and time frames.

✦ CHARACTER LETTER
Pupils write a letter as a character from a studied text. They
could write it to a member of the class who would respond
in turn as a different character, possibly from the same
author. For example, a letter from Bilbo Baggins to Gandalf
regarding events since The Hobbit. Alternatively, children
could write to the Queen or Prime Minister in character
addressing any concerns the character may have. A different
pupil could then respond in turn.

✦ OBITUARY
Write the obituary for a character in the story. Include their entire lifespan, background, etc.

✦ INTERVIEW
Two options are available depending upon the availability of recording equipment:

❒ Prepare written questions for an interview and then record the responses. These could then be added to the retyped questions and presented as a magazine style interview.

❒ Pupils prepare a series of written questions they would like to ask a character. Pupils exchange questions and write written responses to them in the character they have been allocated.

167. **Creative writing starting points**

What you need: optional use of laptops
Subject links: literacy, ICT

✦ ADD A CHARACTER
Rewrite a well-known tale with the addition of one additional character who will transform the story line, eg Sleeping Beauty when a Tardis and Dr Who materialize, or Tracey Beaker in a WW2 scenario. Add only one character. This exercise could be extended to initiate discussion about the impact a single person can have on events around him/her.

✦ MISSING NARRATIVE
Give pupils a section of dialogue from a text. Pupils must expand the story, determining what events or actions take place in between the dialogue provided in the extract. Optionally, provide a cut and paste copy of the dialogue in chronological order for pupils to cut and glue into their stories. This could be as a word document for use on computers or as a paper copy.

✦ SENTENCE PARTNERS
Pupils create a written document with a partner. Each take it in turns to write a sentence. They continue until the task is finished and then edit their work together.

✦ SETTING SENSES
Use the five senses to create a web for the setting to draw out the details. If pupils state a particular feature, they must include why, eg dark – caused by towering cliffs looming over the canyon.

✦   SHARED WRITING ACROSS YEAR GROUPS
Pupils write for an audience of younger learners. The younger class may have had the opportunity to choose the theme and style of writing themselves. The older children need to be selective in their choice of words, length of sentences and clarity of plot. If possible, swap with the other year's class teacher who would introduce the session to the older children and reinforce the level of writing for the target audience.

✦   STREAM OF CONSCIOUSNESS
Pupils write continuously for a set period of up to five minutes. They must keep writing all the time and, if they have a mental block, simply keep repeating their last word.

✦   After the set time limit, pupils count the total number of words and delete half of the original number, especially repetition or boring words. Repeat this process , cutting the word number again by half. Use this remnant as the core for a piece of creative or poetic writing.

Numeracy

168. **Market research**

What you need: access to Excel, PowerPoint, Word or similar
Subject links: numeracy, literacy, ICT

✦ The class conducts market research to produce a planned investigation (what do they want or need to find out). Prepare practice questions to discover information and show the results from the research in a spreadsheet and/or graph format.

✦ Pupils present the meaning behind their findings to the class in the format of PowerPoint presentations. This may take two or more lessons to complete depending on the depth of research and the pupils' familiarity with the software.

Geography

169. **Local improvements**

What you need: maps, paper, rulers, colour pencils, playground resource/wildlife/ outdoor classroom catalogues
Subject links: geography, PSHE, literacy

✦ Pupils investigate what could be done to improve a run-down area of the school or an area close to the school. Using geographical terms, pupils could record its current state using mapping and cameras. Develop a sense of scale. Using school catalogues or garden catalogues, pupils could investigate the possibilities of developing the site into a play or study/wildlife area. Pupils could create a written chart with two columns, recording problems on the one side and solutions on the other.

✦ These suggestions together with a view of possible equipment that may be purchased could be detailed into an affirmative letter or proposal for the school or local council to investigate and explore.

170. **Urban v rural**

What you need: paper, pens
Subject links: geography

✦ Create a contrast chart plotting the advantages and disadvantages of rural and urban living. Pupils compare the two and provide an informed geographical reason for their preference for rural or urban living.

171. **PE map**

What you need: paper, pencils, ruler, prior awareness of PE skills to be acquired and equipment to be used

Subject links: geography, PE

✦　Pupils may either draw a map of the hall or playground that will be used during a PE lesson or, alternatively, they may be provided with a plan to complete. Pupils should add details to the map and show the location of resources to be used, along with the learning objective of the lesson they wish to create.

✦　Remind pupils to incorporate safety within their plans. Pupils engage in higher order thinking to reason how and why the equipment should be located or utilized. They should be able to explain to the teacher or class why and how their plan would work for this lesson. Ideally, this activity should be done prior to a PE lesson, allowing the best ideas to be used by the class.

172. **Playground map**

What you need: playground plan, colours, possible use of timers
Subject links: geography, PSHE, school council

✦ Encourage pupils to think about how and why a location is used as well as how to record people's behaviour visually. Concentrating upon the school playground, aim to show pupil/staff distribution, use of space, location of activities, outdoor equipment use, etc. Create a key to record the information.

✦ For higher order thinking, encourage explanations for use of space to be reached following the data capture. Why do certain activities take place predominately in certain areas? Ideally, complete the data capture by allocating pupils five-minute time slots, so that the whole lunch hour is covered. This could be followed by class analysis and discussion during the afternoon whilst memories are still fresh. Discuss finding solutions to areas of crowding or better use of low-access areas.

✦ Create a class map for the school council to show how the area could be improved at lunchtime to promote better and healthier behaviour.

History

173. **What happens next?**

What you need: CD, textual account or web video of dramatic event
Subject links: geography, history, RE, speaking and listening

✦   Read or play an audio account of the beginning of a dramatic event.

✦   Read or play it three times to the class. Pupils should use the evidence and their imagination and existing knowledge to deduce what could happen next. Emphasize using the five senses to engage them in the event.

✦   Plenary: replay for the final time followed by pupils reading their accounts of the outcome.

174. **Rules**

What you need: topic knowledge
Subject links: history, RE

✦   Write down some of the rules of the culture being studied.

✦   Pupils could discuss or write the following questions: Why do you think they have these rules? Do we follow any of these rules today in our culture? Do you follow any of these rules yourself?

175. **Past lives**
What you need: prior topic awareness and reference materials
Subject links: history, literacy, RE

✦ JOB DESCRIPTION
Pupils write a job description for a role studied. Include the job title, job description, age required, character or personality needed, pay, skills, power, holidays and any dangers or perks.

✦ MASTER OF CEREMONIES
Plan a day or evening of entertainment for an important historical figure or character. What would it involve? Who, what, when, where, etc. This exercise is most suited for the leisure habits of kings and rulers.

✦ MEET THE DEAD
Who would you like to meet and why? What questions would you ask? What would you like to do with them? How would you dress, eat and travel together?

176. **Topical music**
What you need: music linked to a historical/geographical topic
Subject links: history, geography, music, literacy

✦ Pupils listen to music from another historical or geographical culture and record their thoughts on what the music is about. Encourage them to use expressive language to draw out the impact of the music. For some sounds that are very different to Western ears it may help to state what the music is, prior to playing. Many tracks from other cultures, past and present, can now be downloaded.

✦ Pupils could also create a simple piece of music to illustrate or accompany a character from a text or to illustrate a scene with appropriate purpose and emotion.

RE

177. **Our prayer**
What you need: nothing
Subject links: RE

✦ Pupils write out their own prayers as individuals, pairs or as a group. Encourage the use of different genres, such as rap, poem, haiku, tanka, lyric, etc, as a means of expressing inner thoughts and feelings.

✦ Try to ensure that the emphasis is not upon correct literary technique but is upon expressing a personal prayer supported by these structures.

PSHE

178. **Goal setting**
What you need: paper, pens
Subject links: PSHE

✦ Pupils write down goals that they wish to achieve today, this week, this term, this year and as an adult. Model how to break down into small stages the process of moving towards completion. Focus upon bite-sized do-able actions that could be followed as stepping stones towards achieving the longer term goals.

Subject index

Art, Design and Technology

Activity no.

4 Advertising
154 Board game
36 Co-ordinates symmetrical mask
13 Create a dictionary
158 Fact, opinion or belief?
101 Fractions
31 Giving instructions
44 Historical maps
43 History pictorial activities
58 Identifying key features
18 Inspiring creative writing
75 Instructions
106 Life-sized paper skeleton
124 Mistakes
92 Model making
89 Mr Men™ books
28 Picture that!
27 Posters
67 Prayer
7 Quick quiz
150 Setting goals and providing feedback
26 Ticket design
11 Topic book
72 Visual healthy menu
48 When they were young

Geography

80 3-D Carroll diagrams
4 Advertising
154 Board game
57 Choropleth map
6 Classification keys
62 Cloud survey
114 Compass bearings
13 Create a dictionary
32 Digital storyboard
10 Encyclopedic entry
135 Envoy
61 Estate agent
8 Freeze frame
157 Gathering information
113 Geography Twister®
79 Getting out of the classroom
64 Global food
44 Historical maps
43 History pictorial activities
60 Holiday destinations
127 Hot seat mind map
45 House comparison
58 Identifying key features
112 Inflatable globes
75 Instructions
115 International sign posts
9 Kim's game
110 Kineasthetic history ideas

73 Lifestyle map
128 Listening, writing and speaking games
169 Local improvements
53 Local or world/national picture maps
94 Lost
145 Map symbol snap
63 Micro water cycle
124 Mistakes
92 Model making
129 Name hat
59 Photo record
28 Picture that!
172 Playground map
27 Posters
3 Presenting facts
153 Questions
7 Quick quiz
20 Reports and reviews
46 Rich/poor comparison chart
82 Sequencing
150 Setting goals and providing feedback
81 Sorting ideas
126 Speaking challenges
151 Speaking games
55 Sports map
155 Storytelling and debating
5 Structure grids
65 Symbol and word match cards
56 Task map

Teaching Boys in Primary School

122 Team raps and poems
76 Thought lines
11 Topic book
123 Topic singing
176 Topical music
146 Treasure hunt
47 TV news
170 Urban v rural
54 Virtual maps
12 Visual literacy skills
1 Visual word games
83 Washing line
173 What happens next?
111 What really happened?
48 When they were young
130 Word pairs

History

80 3-D Carroll diagrams
4 Advertising
51 Alphabets
40 Ancient Egyptian multiplication
154 Board game
16 Character grids
17 Character work
6 Classification keys
13 Create a dictionary
32 Digital storyboard
10 Encyclopedic entry
61 Estate agent
135 Envoy
158 Fact, opinion or belief?
8 Freeze frame
166 Get to know your character
152 Group discussion
44 Historical maps
50 Historical timetable
43 History pictorial activities
127 Hot seat mind map
45 House comparison
58 Identifying key features
75 Instructions
93 Investigating characters
9 Kim's game
110 Kineasthetic history ideas
128 Listening, writing and speaking games
53 Local or world/national picture maps
74 Mime
124 Mistakes
92 Model making
129 Name hat
175 Past lives
49 Personal and class timelines
28 Picture that!
27 Posters
3 Presenting facts
153 Questions
7 Quick quiz
46 Rich/poor comparison chart
30 Role-playing
39 Roman times tables
174 Rules
52 Scribe a letter
82 Sequencing
150 Setting goals and providing feedback
126 Speaking challenges
151 Speaking games
81 Sorting ideas
155 Storytelling and debating
5 Structure grids
65 Symbol and word match cards
122 Team raps and poems
76 Thought lines
11 Topic book
123 Topic singing
176 Topical music
47 TV news
12 Visual literacy skills
1 Visual word games
83 Washing line
173 What happens next?
111 What really happened?
48 When they were young
130 Word pairs

ICT

68 Action
4 Advertising
32 Digital storyboard
24 Film education
166 Get to know your character
33 Hyperlink PowerPoint
18 Inspiring creative writing

168 Market research
124 Mistakes
71 Personal timetable
27 Posters
3 Presenting facts
20 Reports and reviews
69 Role models
156 Soundtrack
155 Storytelling and debating
11 Topic book
47 TV news

Language and Literacy

Reading

90 Book swap cirlce
131 Book team
31 Giving instructions
132 Land's End to John O'Groats reading race
124 Mistakes
92 Model making
21 Newspaper headline: sort and match
22 Newspapers/web news comparison
161 Personal responses
163 Prediction
133 Races
30 Role-playing
82 Sequencing
5 Structure grids
12 Visual literacy skills
1 Visual word games

Speaking and Listening

80 3-D Carroll diagrams
4 Advertising
164 Alternative scene
159 Ask the author
90 Book swap circle
16 Character grids
17 Character work
23 Comparative news
135 Envoy
158 Fact, opinion or belief?
24 Film education
84 Fun spelling
157 Gathering information
79 Getting out of the classroom
152 Group discussion
127 Hot seat mind map
58 Identifying key features
75 Instructions
9 Kim's game
110 Kineasthetic history ideas
128 Listening, writing and speaking games
94 Lost
100 Magic chairs
168 Market research
25 Media and plays
74 Mime
124 Mistakes
129 Name hat
77 Name game
22 Newspaper/web news comparison
175 Past lives
161 Personal responses
2 Pictorial activities
28 Picture that!
163 Prediction
3 Presenting facts
153 Questions
7 Quick quiz
42 Recount
20 Reports and reviews
87 Role-play
30 Role-playing
134 Secret definition
150 Setting goals and providing feedback
29 Show me
126 Speaking challenges
151 Speaking games
81 Sorting ideas
156 Soundtrack
155 Storytelling and debating
88 Student sculpture
103 Team clocks
122 Team raps and poems
160 Text discussion
76 Thought lines
26 Ticket design
123 Topic singing
176 Topical music
47 TV news
54 Virtual maps
12 Visual literacy skills
83 Washing line
173 What happens next?
111 What really happened?
130 Word pairs
162 Wrong reading

Teaching Boys in Primary School

Writing

86 Adjective word bank
165 Alternative versions
154 Board game
15 Book review
16 Character grids
17 Character work
6 Classification keys
23 Comparative news
13 Create a dictionary
167 Creative writing starting points
34 Different perspectives
32 Digital storyboard
10 Encyclopedic entry
61 Estate agent
24 Film education
8 Freeze frame
84 Fun spelling
166 Get to know your character
79 Getting out of the classroom
31 Giving instructions
43 History pictorial activities
33 Hyperlink PowerPoint
19 Information book sections
18 Inspiring creative writing
93 Investigating characters
110 Kinaesthetic history ideas
169 Local improvements
41 Line graph narrative
25 Media and plays
92 Model making
89 Mr Men™ books
21 Newspaper headline: sort and match
175 Past lives
27 Posters
91 Product review
42 Recount
20 Reports and reviews
87 Role-play
30 Role-playing
52 Scribe a letter
128 Setting goals and providing feedback
156 Soundtrack
155 Storytelling and debating
85 Tactile words
160 Text discussion
26 Ticket design
11 Topic book
1 Visual word games
48 When they were young
125 Word and time boundary
14 Word banks

MFL

154 Board game
66 Body and clothes beetle drive
6 Classification keys
142 Colour 'fruit'
13 Create a dictionary
32 Digital storyboard
135 Envoy
79 Getting out of the classroom
43 History pictorial activities
75 Instructions
116 Kineasthetic MFL ideas
144 Last man standing
128 Listening, writing and speaking games
143 MFL faces
139 MFL ideas
140 MFL noughts and crosses
117 MFL Twister®
74 Mime
124 Mistakes
129 Name hat
141 Numbers, colours, shapes and letters
27 Posters
153 Questions
7 Quick quiz
30 Role-playing
150 Setting goals and providing feedback
81 Sorting ideas
126 Speaking challenges
65 Symbol and word match cards
122 Team raps and poems
11 Topic book
47 TV news
12 Visual literacy skills
1 Visual word games
83 Washing line
130 Word pairs

Music

6 Classification keys
124 Mistakes
153 Questions
150 Setting goals and providing feedback
126 Speaking challenges
155 Storytelling and debating
65 Symbol and word match cards
122 Team raps and poems
123 Topic singing
176 Topical music

Numeracy

Calculating

40 Ancient Egyptian multiplication
37 Digital root patterns
136 Football pitch multiplication
39 Roman times tables
38 Times table graphs
99 Times table stand up factors

Counting

138 Number line: connect 3
137 Physical pairs
35 Play your cards right
83 Washing line

Handling data

6 Classification keys
50 Historical timetable
49 Personal and class timelines
71 Personal timetable
103 Team clocks

Knowing number facts

101 Fractions
124 Mistakes
65 Symbol and word match cards

Measurement

104 Axis co-ordinates Twister®
114 Compass bearings
36 Co-ordinates symmetrical mask
107 Earth, Moon and Sun
101 Fractions
115 International signposts
73 Lifestyle map
102 Step estimation
96 Team angles

Understanding shape

98 Kineasthetic patterns
97 Shape creation
81 Sorting ideas

Using and Applying Maths

80 3-D Carroll diagrams
154 Board game
79 Getting out of the classroom
128 Listening, writing and speaking games
100 Magic chairs
168 Market research
129 Name hat
153 Questions
7 Quick quiz
95 Shape maths
126 Speaking challenges
122 Team raps and poems
123 Topic singing
12 Visual literacy skills

Physical Education

119 Instant PE lesson
75 Instructions
128 Listening, writing and speaking games
147 Magic stick
124 Mistakes
171 PE map
120 PE science
118 Physical prayer
3 Presenting facts
42 Recount
20 Reports and reviews
148 Roll out
82 Sequencing
150 Setting goals and providing feedback
126 Speaking challenges
146 Treasure hunt

Teaching Boys in Primary School

PHSE

80 3-D Carroll diagrams
68 Action
4 Advertising
154 Board game
6 Classification keys
32 Digital storyboard
135 Envoy
158 Fact, opinion or belief?
8 Freeze frame
121 Friendly words
157 Gathering information
79 Getting out of the classroom
178 Goal setting
152 Group discussion
149 Head down, thumbs up
43 History pictorial activities
127 Hot seat mind map
58 Identifying key features
75 Instructions
73 Lifestyle map
128 Listening, writing and speaking games
169 Local improvements
147 Magic stick
74 Mime
124 Mistakes
89 Mr Men™ books
129 Name hat
71 Personal timetable
172 Playground map
70 Positive words
27 Posters
3 Presenting facts

153 Questions
69 Role models
87 Role-play
78 Secret whiteboards
82 Sequencing
150 Setting goals and providing feedback
81 Sorting ideas
126 Speaking challenges
151 Speaking games
5 Structure grids
88 Student sculpture
65 Symbol and word match cards
122 Team raps and poems
76 Thought lines
11 Topic book
123 Topic singing
47 TV news
12 Visual literacy skills
72 Visual healthy menu
1 Visual word games
83 Washing line

Religious Education

80 3-D Carroll diagrams
68 Action
154 Board game
16 Character grids
17 Character work
6 Classification keys
13 Create a dictionary
32 Digital storyboard
10 Encyclopedic entry
135 Envoy
158 Fact, opinion or belief?
8 Freeze frame
121 Friendly words
166 Get to know your character
152 Group discussion
43 History pictorial activities
127 Hot seat mind map
58 Identifying key features
75 Instructions
93 Investigating characters
128 Listening, writing and speaking games
74 Mime
124 Mistakes
92 Model making
129 Name hat
177 Our prayer
118 Physical prayer
28 Picture that!
3 Presenting facts
7 Quick quiz
175 Past lives
70 Positive words
27 Posters
67 Prayer
153 Questions
20 Reports and reviews
30 Role-playing
174 Rules
52 Scribe a letter
82 Sequencing
150 Setting goals and providing feedback

81 Sorting ideas
126 Speaking challenges
151 Speaking games
155 Storytelling and debating
5 Structure grids
65 Symbol and word match cards
122 Team raps and poems
76 Thought lines
11 Topic book
123 Topic singing
47 TV news
12 Visual literacy skills
1 Visual word games
83 Washing line
173 What happens next?
111 What really happened?
48 When they were young

Science

Life processes
6 Classification keys
13 Create a dictionary
108 Exploring nature
109 Junior field studies
106 Life-sized paper skeleton

128 Listening, writing and speaking games
81 Sorting ideas
72 Visual healthy menu
1 Visual word games

Materials
6 Classification keys
81 Sorting ideas
105 Transparent, translucent and opaque
1 Visual word games

Physical processes
6 Classification keys
107 Earth, Moon and Sun
63 Micro water cycle
120 PE science
81 Sorting ideas
1 Visual word games

Scientific enquiry
80 3-D Carroll diagrams
154 Board game
6 Classification keys
32 Digital storyboard
10 Encyclopedic entry
135 Envoy
158 Fact, opinion or belief?

79 Getting out of the classroom
152 Group discussion
127 Hot seat mind map
58 Identifying key features
75 Instructions
41 Line graph narrative
128 Listening, writing and speaking games
124 Mistakes
129 Name hat
59 Photo record
3 Presenting facts
153 Questions
7 Quick quiz
42 Recount
150 Setting goals and providing feedback
81 Sorting ideas
126 Speaking challenges
155 Storytelling and debating
5 Structure grids
122 Team raps and poems
76 Thought lines
11 Topic book
123 Topic singing
1 Visual word games
83 Washing line

Teaching Boys in Primary School